Master the SPaG basics with CGP!

This Foundation Question Book from CGP is perfect for helping pupils aged 10-11 get to grips with English in Year 6.

It's bursting with practice questions to help pupils improve the essential grammar, punctuation and spelling skills they'll need.

Each topic starts with helpful examples and there are answers to every question at the back of the book!

What CGP is all about

Our sole aim here at CGP is to produce the highest quality books
— carefully written, immaculately presented
and dangerously close to being funny.

Then we work our socks off to get them out to you
— at the cheapest possible prices.

Contents

Grammar

Section 1 — Word Types

Section 2 — Clauses and Sentences

Section 3 — Linking Ideas

Section 4 — Tenses

Section 5 — Sentence Structure

Section 6 — Writing Style

Punctuation

Section 7 — Sentence Punctuation

Section 8 — Commas

Section 9 — Brackets and Dashes

Section 10 — Apostrophes

Section 11 — Inverted Commas

Section 12 — Colons and Semi-Colons

Contents

Spelling

Published by CGP

Editors
Heather Cowley, Melissa Gardner, Gabrielle Richardson, Hannah Roscoe, Sean Walsh
With thanks to James Summersgill and Alison Griffin for the proofreading.
With thanks to Jan Greenway for the copyright research.
Thumb illustration used throughout the book © iStock.com.
The Grammar and Punctuation sections contain public sector information licensed under the Open Government Licence v3.0.
http://www.nationalarchives.gov.uk/doc/open-government-licence/version/3/

ISBN: 978 1 78908 336 1

Clipart from Corel®
Printed by Elanders Ltd, Newcastle upon Tyne.
Based on the classic CGP style created by Richard Parsons.
Text, design, layout and original illustrations © Coordination Group Publications Ltd. (CGP) 2019
All rights reserved.

Section 1 — Word Types

Nouns

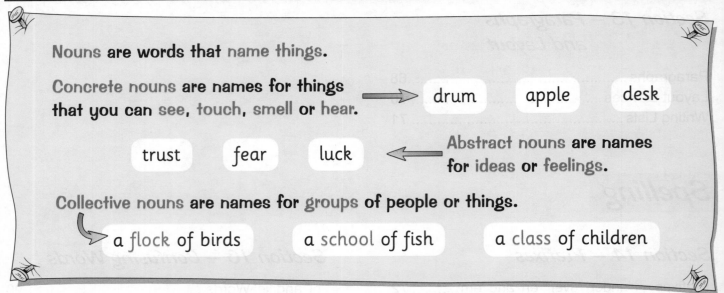

Nouns are words that name things.

Concrete nouns are names for things that you can see, touch, smell or hear. → drum   apple   desk

trust   fear   luck ← Abstract nouns are names for ideas or feelings.

Collective nouns are names for groups of people or things.

a flock of birds   a school of fish   a class of children

---

1 Underline the **abstract nouns** below. Then write them on the **board**.

love   pencil   pain

leaf

car   kindness

joy

bottle   rabbit   peace

---

2 Underline the **collective nouns** in the sentences below.

The pride of lions were lying lazily in the sunshine.

A fleet of ships sailed from England to Africa.

At the nature reserve, a herd of deer ran past me very quickly.

The children were chased by an angry swarm of bees.

"I can identify different types of nouns."

Adjectives

Adjectives are words that tell us **more** about a **noun**.

> a dirty plate   a small shoe   the noisy children

1 | Underline the <u>adjectives</u> in the sentences below.

My grandad baked a delicious cake yesterday.

I bought some fluffy slippers to wear at home.

Matthew found muddy boots in the hallway.

Marina borrowed Shauna's glittery pencil case.

The food was cold and people complained.

The hungry football players ate burgers for dinner.

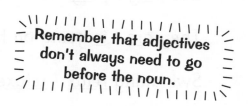

Remember that adjectives don't always need to go before the noun.

2 | Add <u>adjectives</u> to the sentences below.
Use the pictures to help you.

The .... witches were stirring the potion.

The diners complimented the chef on his .... food.

The lady wore a .... scarf to go sledging.

My .... coat got .... in the rain.

"I know what adjectives are and how to use them."

Verbs

Verbs **are** doing or being words. ➡ Abed tells stories.

Verbs change depending on who is doing the action.

I race snails.   She races snails.

Irregular verbs change in different ways. E.g. 'I am', 'you are', 'he/she is'.

(1) **Circle the correct form of each verb to finish these sentences.**

Zoë play / plays in the park every weekend.

They are / is going on holiday to Spain.

Swimming relax / relaxes me after school.

The dogs chases / chase the rabbits around the garden.

When my dad goes to work, he always forget / forgets his lunch.

(2) **Tick the sentences below that use verbs correctly.**

Genevieve has to records a video for her English homework. ☐

We learn how to do gymnastics in P.E. ☐

Mr Lewis teaches us about poems. ☐

I think that chemistry are an exciting subject. ☐

They have to draw pictures to give to their parents. ☐

Marvin drink orange juice for breakfast. ☐

"I know what verbs are and how to use them."

Adverbs

Adverbs **are words that describe** verbs, adjectives **and other adverbs.**

He carefully writes his name.

Martha chews really loudly.

'carefully' is
the adverb

The basement is very cold.

Some adverbs **show how** possible **or** certain **something is.**

probably   definitely   never

1   Choose a suitable <u>adverb</u> from the box to complete each sentence below.

> nervously   much   extremely   suddenly   loudly

Only use each
adverb once.

Margot was .... pleased with her results.

Harry bit his lip .... as he looked at the damage.

The ice cream van plays its music very ....

The opera singer got .... louder as she sang.

The music stopped .... and everyone sat down.

2   Fill in the gaps with either '<u>probably</u>', '<u>never</u>' or '<u>definitely</u>'.

Paul .... eats white chocolate because he doesn't like it.

I love going to the cinema, so I will .... go with you tonight.

Maria said that she will .... come, but she's not sure yet.

"I know what adverbs are and how to use them."

Modal Verbs

Some verbs are used to give more information about the main verb in a sentence. Modal verbs often show how certain or possible something is.

| We might eat cake. | We shall eat cake. | We must eat cake. |
| We would eat cake. | We will eat cake. | We should eat cake. |

1 Tick the sentences that contain **modal verbs**.

I want to go to the cinema tonight.

He would not come to the party on his own.

Shanice may be able to join us later.

Henrietta is not going to share her sweets.

We should go downstairs and set the table.

They must ring the hotel immediately.

2 Underline the **modal verbs** in the sentences below.
Then write them on the **board**.

The plumber should fix the radiators.

We might go to the rock concert this weekend.

I could win the race if I train hard enough.

She must answer the phone when it rings.

We will tell the waiter about your allergies.

3 Circle the correct <u>modal verbs</u> to complete the sentences below.

If you are not sure, you <u>shall</u> / <u>could</u> ask your teacher.

I <u>should</u> / <u>will</u> wash my hair but I have run out of shampoo.

The zebras <u>might</u> / <u>must</u> run quickly to escape the lions.

You <u>must</u> / <u>can</u> go climbing if you tidy your room first.

You <u>might</u> / <u>should</u> always put sun cream on at the beach.

It <u>might</u> / <u>shall</u> rain this weekend, but I am not sure.

4 Write a <u>sentence</u> of your own using each of the <u>modal verbs</u> below. The first one has been done for you.

Look back at the examples and other exercises to help you.

will

The shop will close for three weeks.

....

should

....

must

....

might

....

"I can identify modal verbs and use them correctly."

Synonyms

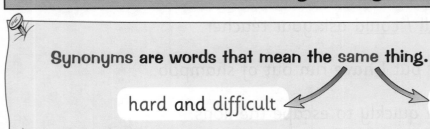

Synonyms are words that mean the same thing.

hard **and** difficult ⟵ ⟶ fast **and** quick

1 Draw lines to match the <u>synonyms</u>.

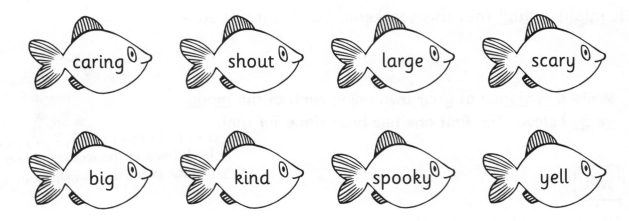

caring   shout   large   scary

big   kind   spooky   yell

2 For each sentence, circle the <u>synonym</u> of the word in bold.

pleased ⟹ My mum is <u>happy</u> / <u>angry</u> about winning the raffle.

upset ⟹ I was really <u>nervous</u> / <u>sad</u> about losing my shoes.

normal ⟹ It was just a <u>special</u> / <u>typical</u> day at school.

3 Write a <u>synonym</u> on the dotted line for each word below.

noisy ⟹ ....   laugh ⟹ ....

tasty ⟹ ....   neat ⟹ ....

"I know what synonyms are and how to use them."

Antonyms

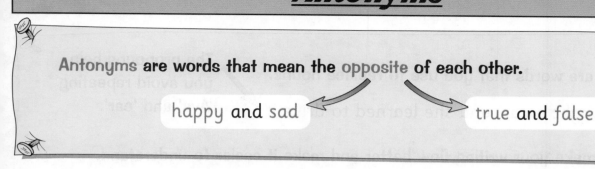

Antonyms are words that mean the opposite of each other.

happy and sad → ← true and false

(1) Draw lines to match the **antonyms**.

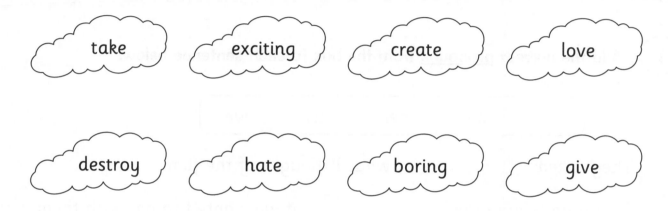

take   exciting   create   love

destroy   hate   boring   give

(2) Add the **correct** word from the box to the sentences below.

~~mean / friendly~~   straight / twisty

brave / cowardly   generous / greedy

My brother makes friends with anyone — he's so ....friendly........... .

I felt car sick because the road was ....

He was really .... — he should have owned up.

She was very .... and shared her lunch with me.

Pronouns

Pronouns are words that you use to replace nouns.

Ava bought a car, and she learned to drive it.

The pronouns help you avoid repeating 'Ava' and 'car'.

They can make your writing flow better and make it easier to understand.

There's Luca's sister. She's taller than him.

'She' refers to Luca's sister and 'him' refers to Luca.

1 Add the correct <u>pronouns</u> from the box to each sentence below.

it	me	her	us	we

They asked .... what I thought of the film.

Sunita and Tom asked .... if we wanted to eat with them.

The kind ladies asked if .... needed any help.

I need my hammer but I can't find .... in the shed.

Lima wanted me to help .... bake chocolate brownies.

2 Rewrite each sentence, replacing the <u>underlined nouns</u> with <u>pronouns</u>.

Clara likes cheese, so <u>Clara</u> eats a lot of <u>cheese</u>.

....

After Elijah ripped the curtains, <u>Elijah</u> tried to fix <u>the curtains</u>.

....

"I know what pronouns are and how to use them."

Relative Pronouns

Relative pronouns **are words like 'who', 'which' and 'whose'.**
They are used to **join** parts of **sentences together.**

The police found the thief who had stolen my bike.	'who' is used for people

I found the photo album which I had lost.	'which' is used for things

(1) Draw lines to complete the sentences using the **relative pronouns**.

She found an old car   won the award.

We met the actress   **which**   was very rusty.

Shirley baked a cake   is a firefighter.

I have a friend    **who**   contained nuts and coffee.

(2) Use a **relative pronoun** from the box to complete each sentence below.

who   whose   which

I bought a jumper .... was brightly coloured.

There is a bookshop in town .... opens on Sundays.

Tahani adopted a cat .... owner had left him.

The winner is someone .... has worked very hard.

"I know how to use relative pronouns."

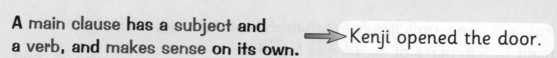

Clauses

A main clause has a subject and a verb, and makes sense on its own. ⟶ Kenji opened the door.

A subordinate clause gives extra information, but doesn't make sense on its own.

Kenji opened the door because the bell rang.

main clause   subordinate clause

A relative clause is a type of subordinate clause. It is often introduced by a relative pronoun.

Relative pronouns are words like 'that', 'which', 'whose' and 'who'.

Jules had a friend who played tennis.

relative pronoun   relative clause

1 Draw lines to match each group of words to the **correct** label.

because it was wet   he was in a play

she read a book   **main clause**   if they don't watch

we baked a cake   they sold the painting

after it was over   while they sang

who was funny   **subordinate clause**   I went to France

2 Underline the **subordinate clause** in each sentence below.

They're making a curry because it's their favourite meal.

Chidi has two black labradors which are really friendly.

After the concert ends, we're going to buy some ice-cream.

I'd like to go for a walk tomorrow even if it's raining.

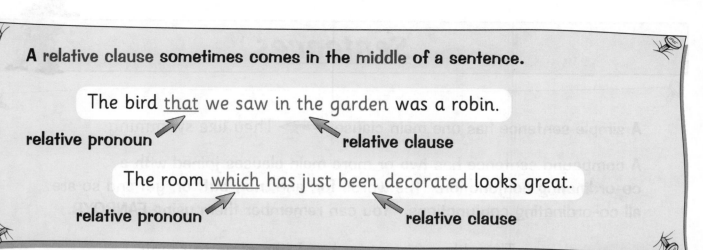

A relative clause sometimes comes in the middle of a sentence.

The bird <u>that</u> we saw in the garden was a robin.

relative pronoun   relative clause

The room <u>which</u> has just been decorated looks great.

relative pronoun   relative clause

3)   Underline the <u>relative clause</u> in each of the sentences below.

Ellen, who wants to be a doctor, is going to medical school.

The museum that stays open at night is very popular.

The programme that the toddlers were watching was a cartoon.

My friend, who is called Matt, fell into the pond.

The old man who lives down the road used to be an actor.

4)   Add a <u>relative clause</u> from the box to the sentences below.

> which looks like a bear   who works in the local café
> that I made with my friend   who loves animals

The chef .... cooked some ham.

The kite .... blew into a tree.

Jeremy's brother .... went to the zoo.

The statue .... had fallen over.

"I can spot main, subordinate and relative clauses."

     Section 2 — Clauses and Sentences

Sentences

A simple sentence **has** one main clause. → They like swimming.

A compound sentence **has two or more** main clauses **joined with a co-ordinating conjunction. The words** for, and, nor, but, or, yet **and** so **are all co-ordinating conjunctions. You can remember them using FANBOYS.**

They like swimming, but I like playing tennis.

main clause   co-ordinating conjunction   main clause

1   **Write S for simple sentence or C for compound sentence next to the sentences below.**

Neve took the train down to London. ☐

We went to the shop and I bought some sweets. ☐

Mr and Mrs Adler just moved in next door. ☐

I can't dive, but I want to have some lessons. ☐

Isaac was cold, so he put his coat on. ☐

2   **Use the conjunctions in the boxes to turn each pair of sentences into one compound sentence.**

[so]   We were hungry. We cooked a stew.

....

[and]   Jaya walked to the beach. She went surfing.

....

[but]   They wanted to play. The park was shut.

....

A **complex sentence** has a **main clause** and one or more **subordinate clauses**.

The clauses are linked by a **subordinating conjunction**, which can go at the **start** or in the **middle** of the sentence.

subordinating → <u>After</u> I play tennis, I always eat a banana.
conjunction

subordinate clause   main clause

3 Draw lines to match each sentence to the **correct** label.

They went sailing on the boat.

Even though I was tired, I went to see my friend.

Margot's uncle is moving to America.

He was lost, so he asked for directions.

We could read or we could watch TV.

As we watched, the frog jumped out of the pond.

simple

compound

complex

4 Write a **simple**, a **compound** and a **complex** sentence about the picture below.

Simple ⟹ ....

Compound ⟹ ....

....

Complex ⟹ ....

....

"I can use simple, compound and complex sentences."

Section 3 — Linking Ideas

Conjunctions

Conjunctions **are words or phrases that** join two sentences **or** two parts **of a sentence. They help your writing to** flow smoothly.

My friend was late. We missed the bus. I called a taxi. ← **This** doesn't flow very well.

My friend was late and we missed the bus, so I called a taxi.

This flows much better.

1   **Choose the correct <u>conjunction</u> to complete each sentence. Use each word only <u>once</u>.**

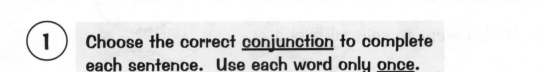

because   and   but   so

Anisa ate a banana .... she was hungry.

The milk was out of date, ... Jo went to the shop.

The family went to theatre .... had a great time.

I wanted to go to the zoo, ... it was closed.

2   **Join the sentences below using either '<u>but</u>' or '<u>so</u>'.**

Marcel likes broccoli. He doesn't like mushrooms.

....

There was a storm. We didn't go sailing.

....

"I can link ideas together using conjunctions."   

Linking Paragraphs

Adverbial phrases **tell you** how, when, where **or** how often **something happens.**
They can also be used to link sentences **and** paragraphs **together.**

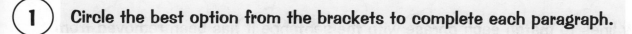

We played on the swings. After a while, we went for a walk.

The adverbial phrase **helps these** sentences **to flow.**

1 Circle the best option from the brackets to complete each paragraph.

It's very important to eat well and spend time relaxing.

(<u>Similarly</u> / <u>Firstly</u>), eating healthily means that your body is being

looked after from the inside. If you eat well, you will have lots of energy.

(<u>Also</u> / <u>However</u>), don't forget to treat yourself every now and then

— it's good for you (not to mention delicious!)

(<u>Secondly</u> / <u>In contrast</u>), taking time to relax and doing the things

you enjoy keeps your mind happy. You should do things that make you

feel positive.

(<u>Last of all</u> / <u>Although</u>), it's important to remember that everyone is

different. Do what works for you — if exercise makes you feel great but

your friend prefers knitting, that's okay!

"I can link paragraphs using adverbial phrases."

Section 3 — Linking Ideas

Using Ellipsis

Ellipsis **means** removing **a word or phrase** which you would expect **to be included in a sentence.** It helps your sentences and paragraphs flow smoothly.

> Fiona plays chess on Wednesdays and she plays chess on Sundays.

'she plays chess on' has been removed. → Fiona plays chess on Wednesdays and Sundays.

---

1 Draw lines to match each **phrase** with the **sentence** it has been **removed from**.

They stayed because they were asked.

Cara went climbing but Taran didn't.

We visited museums in Poland and Hungary.

I like video games but my friends don't.

Kimi and Mike bought a house and a dog.

- we visited museums in
- like video games
- to stay
- they bought
- go climbing

---

2 Underline the **words** or **phrases** which can be **removed** from these sentences.

I need to clean my rugby kit and I need to clean my trainers.

Talib read about the police dogs and he read about their training.

This weekend, we should paint the fences and we should paint the shed.

Sorcha watches programmes about science and programmes about history.

"I can use ellipsis correctly."

Present Tense and Past Tense

To write about something that happens regularly, use the present tense.

> Ali plays football.

> Mum drives to work.

To write about something that's finished, use the past tense.

> Ali played football.

> Mum drove to work.

1 Draw lines to show whether each sentence is in the **present** or the **past tense**.

I bought a new hat for the wedding.

Samir does his homework after dinner.

We listened to our favourite song.

Toby went on holiday to France.

Remi goes to dance class on Tuesdays.

present

past

2 Underline the **present tense** verb in each sentence and then rewrite the sentence in the **past tense**.

Dean <u>watches</u> cartoons. ⟹ ....Dean watched cartoons.....................................

Laura visits the island. ⟹ ....

The dog rolls over. ⟹ ....

I eat lunch at midday. ⟹ ....

We finish at 3 o'clock. ⟹ ....

"I can use the present tense tend the past tense."

Verbs with 'ing'

To write about something that's still happening, use the present form of 'to be' plus the main verb with 'ing' on the end. This is called the present progressive.

are / am / is ➕ verb ➕ ing ➡️ Dana is waiting in line.

'ing' verbs in the past use the past form of 'to be' instead. This is the past progressive. ➡️ Emma was fixing her bike.

1 Form the present tense with 'ing' by using the correct form of 'to be' and the 'ing' form of each verb.

verb	present tense with 'ing'
to swim	Milo ....is swimming........... .
to shout	You .... for Li.
to bake	I .... a pie.
to move	They .... house.
to look	Amy .... for you.

2 Cross out the incorrect words to form the past tense with 'ing'.

I (am / was / were) watching the film.

You (are / is / were) telling the story.

She (is / are / was) taking the bus.

They (was / were / are) singing along.

"I can use the verbs in their 'ing' forms."

Verbs with 'have'

You can use the present form of the verb 'to have' to talk about something that happened recently.

> The traffic light has turned red.

This is the present perfect tense.

The verb after 'to have' is often in its past tense form, but not always.

> I have opened the window.

> I have done it.   (not 'I have did it')

1 Underline the correct form of '<u>to have</u>' to form the <u>present perfect</u>.

Dominic (has / have) passed his test.

I (has / have) done my chores.

You (has / have) worked hard.

Riley and Priya (has / have) made clay sculptures.

Maisie (has / have) been in the garden.

2 Rewrite these sentences with the <u>correct form</u> of the <u>verb</u> in <u>brackets</u> to make the present perfect.

Olivia ✚ (to have) ✚ (to ask) to go first.

....

We ✚ (to have) ✚ (to find) the recipe.

....

Hassan ✚ (to have) ✚ (to save) his pocket money.

....

Section 4 — Tenses

You can talk about something that happened
before something else using the past perfect tense.

The traffic light had turned red when the car stopped.

To form this, you need the past form of 'to have'. The verb after
'to have' is often in its past tense form, but not always.

I had looked at it.   I had gone out.   (not 'I had went out')

3 Tick the boxes next to sentences that use the <u>past perfect tense</u>.

Will had received the letter. ☐

I ate breakfast at 8 o'clock. ☐

They had brought a map. ☐

Sofia has won the competition. ☐

I had drawn the picture myself. ☐

Remember — there must be
a past form of 'have' for the
past perfect.

4 Form the <u>past perfect</u> by using the <u>past form</u>
of '<u>to have</u>' and the <u>correct form</u> of each <u>verb</u>.

verb	past perfect
to win	Eva .... had won ....
to stop	They ....
to hurt	He .... his knee.
to throw	She .... the ball.
to miss	Max .... the bus.

"I can use the past and present perfect forms."

Staying in the Same Tense

The verbs in a sentence should usually be in the same tense.

Nia went fishing and she caught a fish. ⟵ past tense sentence

present tense sentence ⟶ When we visit friends, we take them presents.

1 Draw lines between boxes in the <u>same tense</u> to make <u>three sentences</u>.

Dan goes home	because I am not wearing a coat	because they were friends.
I am getting cold	and invited her to his birthday party	before he eats dinner.
Amir rang Lucy	and watches television	even though it is snowing.

2 There are some mistakes in the <u>tenses</u> in the passage below. Circle the verbs that are in the <u>wrong tense</u>, and write the <u>corrections</u> below.

Last summer, I went to the beach and I build a huge sandcastle.

....

I work on it almost all day, although I stop for an ice-cream

....

at lunchtime. Afterwards, the tide came in and knocks it down!

....

"I can stay in the right tense in my writing."

Section 5 — Sentence Structure

Subject and Object

A simple sentence has a subject and a verb and it usually has an object.

The subject is the person or thing doing the verb. It usually comes first.

The object usually comes after the verb. It has something done to it by the verb.

The mole | digs | a tunnel.

The verb usually comes after the subject.

This is only true for active sentences. See page 28.

---

1 Underline the **subject** in each of these sentences.

Hanifa goes to school.

The builder bought a ladder.

The bananas changed colour.

Donna made an apple pie.

---

2 Circle the **object** in each of these sentences.

We painted the fences.

I cooked eggs this morning.

Pandas eat bamboo.

Chesleigh climbed the wall.

---

3 Label the **underlined part** of each sentence as either the **subject** or the **object**.

Ben writes <u>a letter</u> to his grandma every Friday. ➡ ....

<u>The lizard</u> ran across the wall. ➡ ....

<u>Dinosaurs</u> walked the Earth millions of years ago. ➡ ....

The tennis player always breaks <u>his racket</u>. ➡ ....

4 Draw lines to complete the sentences and show whether the <u>subject</u> or the <u>object</u> is missing. The first one has been done for you.

Jodie and Paul tidied ....

The parrot repeated ....

.... went to the waterpark.

The cricket players won ....

.... are playful animals.

the question

the match

their rooms

Dolphins

Tony

subject

object

5 Complete each sentence by writing in a <u>subject</u> or an <u>object</u> of your own.

object ⟶ Robbie took .... from his bag.

subject ⟶ .... dropped her phone in the pool.

subject ⟶ .... chased the vampire away.

object ⟶ Sarah played with ....

subject ⟶ .... live in the desert.

object ⟶ They bought .... for the dance.

"I can find the subject and the object in a sentence."

Passive and Active Voice

In active sentences, the subject of the sentence does something to the object.

subject → Imogen lifts weights. ← object

In passive sentences, something is done to the subject.

subject → The weights are lifted by Imogen.

The word 'by' can introduce who does the action.

1 Draw lines to show if the sentences below are <u>active</u> or <u>passive</u>.

The card was written by Tia.   The dog ate her sandwich.

We bought new umbrellas.   active   The bus was delayed by a flood.

The key was lost by Sammy.   passive   He painted the puppets.

Their cat was found by me.   Shane fell in the ditch.

2 Tick the <u>passive</u> sentences below.

The motorcycles were driven by professionals.   ☐

The postman delivered the parcel to the wrong address.   ☐

Pavel planted trees by the river with his friends.   ☐

The dam was built by the beavers.   ☐

Uncle John took the bins out.   ☐

The jumper was knitted by my grandad.   ☐

3 Unscramble the words in each box to write a __passive sentence__.

> Fiona   played   by   guitar   was   the

The guitar was played by Fiona.

....

> pie   was   the   George   by   eaten

....

> was   the   Faisal   delivered   parcel   by

....

> the   was   Wendy   rabbit   adopted   by

....

4 Rewrite each sentence, changing it from __active__ to __passive__.

The firefighter climbed the ladder.

The ladder was climbed by the firefighter.

....

Candice picked the suitcase up.

....

The best athlete won the medal.

....

Kai passed the ball to Hannah.

....

"I can identify active and passive sentences."

Section 6 — Writing Style

Formal and Informal Writing

Formal **words** are used when you're writing something **important**. It can sound quite **serious**.

I am incredibly happy.

Formal **writing** doesn't use apostrophes for shortened versions of words, so you need to say 'I am', not 'I'm'.

Informal **words** are **chattier** and **friendlier**.

I'm over the moon.

Informal **writing** can include shortened versions of words and informal phrases.

1 For each pair of sentences, write **'F'** next to the <u>formal</u> version and **'I'** next to the <u>informal</u> version.

I'm starving. ☐

I am extremely hungry. ☐

Please hurry up. ☐

Just get a move on. ☐

She is annoying me. ☐

She's getting on my nerves. ☐

Take your hands off it! ☐

Do not touch it. ☐

2 Decide if each sentence is <u>formal</u> or <u>informal</u> and draw a line to the correct ring.

Thank you for replying to my letter.

That action film was so cool.

We were gutted with the score.

The test was extremely difficult.

I scoffed all the biscuits.

formal writing

informal writing

Formal **writing** doesn't use exclamation marks. Question marks **can be used as long as the questions are polite.**

> Can I borrow this book?

Some writing uses very formal **sentence structures.**

> If I were you, I would go.

In informal writing, **you'd say 'was' instead of 'were'.**

Informal **writing can include shortened versions of words.**

> They're going to Greece.

Questions are often added to the end of statements in informal writing.

> I can borrow this book, can't I?

3 Draw lines to join each <u>informal</u> sentence with the matching <u>formal</u> one.

That can't be right.

I wish it was that simple.

You're coming, aren't you?

Are you coming?

That cannot be true.

I wish it were that simple.

4 Put a tick next to the <u>formal</u> sentences.

You're always getting at me. ☐

We had an enjoyable day at the beach. ☐

He would play outside if it were warmer. ☐

She will apologise, won't she? ☐

Mark dumped his bags in the hallway. ☐

Nobody believed I would go to the party. ☐

5 For each sentence, circle the more <u>formal</u> word in the brackets.

The food at the restaurant was (rubbish / terrible).

We were all (tired / shattered) after the match.

I saw her (pinch / steal) your pencil case.

He is (bored / sick) of playing that game.

Diego was (eager / itching) to know the answer.

The teacher thought they were (brainy / clever).

6 Complete the crossword by finding a <u>formal</u> word that means the <u>same</u> as the underlined <u>informal</u> word or phrase in each clue.

<u>Across</u>

1. I <u>zoomed</u> across the road.
2. Paul was <u>blubbing</u> after the argument.
3. Lesley <u>chucked</u> the ball at me.

<u>Down</u>

1. She <u>figured</u> they'd forgotten.
2. I <u>lugged</u> the heavy box inside.
3. My best <u>mate</u> lives there.

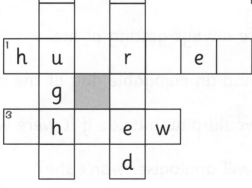

"I can recognise formal and informal vocabulary."

Writing for Your Audience

The audience of a piece of writing is the person or people who read it. Your writing needs to be suitable for that audience.

Formal writing is used for reports, essays and letters to people you don't know.

You should use informal writing when you know the reader, e.g. when writing a letter to a friend.

You should use formal language in most of your writing.

1 **Put a tick next to the formal texts.**

A letter to your local newspaper. ☐

A school report about World War II. ☐

A postcard to your friend telling them about your holiday. ☐

An email to your aunt asking for her advice. ☐

A text message to your mum to say you'll be late home. ☐

2 **Decide if each text would use formal or informal writing and draw a line to the correct sign.**

A thank you note to your uncle.

A science report for school.

A letter to your headteacher.

A party invitation to your friend.

An essay about the Romans.

An email to your cousin.

formal writing

informal writing

3 **Tick the sentence that you would be <u>most likely to find</u> in each text type.**

An article in a newspaper

Police are still looking for the criminal. ☐

The cops still haven't found the crook. ☐

A postcard to your friend

I am having a truly wonderful time. ☐

I'm having an awesome time! ☐

A letter of complaint

I think you should sort it out. ☐

I expect you to fix it. ☐

A note to your dad

I'm sorry for shouting at you. ☐

I apologise for raising my voice. ☐

4 **Tick the sentences that would be <u>most appropriate</u> for the text type below.**

A letter to the Queen

It'd be so good if you came to visit our school. ☐

It would be wonderful if you were to visit our school. ☐

I look forward to hearing from you. ☐

Hope to hear from you soon! ☐

Standard and Non-Standard English

Standard English is correct English. You should use Standard English in your written work. It helps make your writing clearer.

Standard English → | He did it. | Isla and I cheered. | I could have stayed. |

non-Standard English → | He done it. | Me and Isla cheered. | I could of stayed. |

1 Decide if each sentence is <u>Standard</u> or <u>non-Standard English</u> and draw a line to the correct hand.

Clara ran into the garden.

I is not listening anymore.

You done everything wrong.

He is very happy to see you.

We was going to the supermarket.

Those chocolates is very tasty.

I did my homework before going out.

Standard English

non-Standard English

2 Draw lines to match each sentence with its <u>Standard English</u> form.

| She could of come with us. | You would have upset them. |

| You would of upset them. | He should have phoned me. |

| He should of phoned me. | She could have come with us. |

3 Cross out the <u>incorrect options</u> so that each sentence is in <u>Standard English</u>.

I (seen / saw) the dog steal the sausages.

Ben (did / done) all his work.

We (gone / went) out before Lucy arrived.

They (come / came) to the concert last night.

I (drank / drunk) all the milk.

You (swum / swam) further than I did.

4 Draw lines to show which word <u>completes</u> these sentences in <u>Standard English</u>.

I think .... flowers belong to her.

Pick up .... clothes for me.

It was nice of .... to visit us.

She likes .... cakes over there.

Have you told .... the news?

I don't want to talk to ....

them

those

5 Write either '<u>I</u>' or '<u>me</u>' to complete each sentence in <u>Standard English</u>.

Harry got in trouble for hitting ....

I

My friends and .... play hockey.

My brother gave .... this jumper.

me

.... told you not to, but you didn't listen.

In Standard English, only use one negative word to make the meaning negative. ⇒ We can't see.

Double negatives are non-Standard English. ⇒ We can't see nothing.

'Ain't' is non-Standard English. ⇒ I ain't listening.

6 Write '2' next to the <u>double negative</u> sentences and 'l' next to those with <u>one negative</u>.

I haven't eaten nothing today. ☐

Joe didn't see any animals on safari. ☐

I wasn't going to tell nobody. ☐

Kerry couldn't see nothing outside. ☐

I don't have anything to say. ☐

7 Write out each sentence below in <u>Standard English</u>.

It ain't worth it. ....It isn't worth it...

He hasn't seen nobody. ....

They ain't with us. ....

You ain't done nothing. ....

I haven't got no pens. ....

We ain't going to do it. ....

"I feel confident using Standard English in my writing." 👍✓ 🤚✓ 👎✓

Section 7 — Sentence Punctuation

Capital Letters and Full Stops

Sentences always start with a capital letter and often finish with a full stop.
Use capital letters for names of particular people, places or things, and for I.

> Today I am tidying my room.

> Ruby went to France.

1 Put a tick next to the sentences that use <u>capital letters</u> and <u>full stops</u> correctly and put a cross next to the ones that don't.

Jan wants to visit a museum in germany.
☐

my cousin hollie is getting married in may.
☐

Cornwall is a popular holiday destination.
☐

Football and Netball are team Sports
☐

Fleur has lived in both France and England.
☐

2 Rewrite these sentences with <u>capital letters</u> and <u>full stops</u> in the correct places.

jack and kyle skateboard in hyde park

....

elisha is in mrs patel's class next year

....

i have a black and white dog called lola

....

"I can use capital letters and full stops."

Question Marks and Exclamation Marks

Questions always end with a question mark and often begin with a question word. How are you?

Exclamation marks can be used for **commands** or to show when something is said **loudly** or with **strong emotion**. I don't believe it!

---

1 Draw lines to match each sentence to the correct <u>punctuation mark</u>.

What's your favourite colour   Whose shoes are those

Dinner was alright   Who wants to play a game

Can you help me   Our family is quite small

Let's see what happens   Are you finished

I don't know who to ask   We'd better get going now

---

2 Put a <u>full stop</u> or an <u>exclamation mark</u> in each box to complete the sentences.

We're having pizza tonight ☐   Oh, what a beautiful day ☐

Wow, I can't wait ☐   Quick, somebody help me ☐

My socks are green ☐   Pass the sugar, please ☐

---

3 Write a <u>question</u> of your own. Use the picture to help you.

....

"I can use question marks and exclamation marks."

Sentence Practice

Remember — sentences must always start with a capital letter.
They can end with a **full stop**, a **question mark** or an **exclamation mark**.

1 Circle any letters that should be <u>capital letters</u> in the sentences below.

the river in london is called the thames.

wales is a country in great britain.

charles darwin was a famous scientist.

See p.38 for a reminder of when to use a capital letter.

2 Draw lines to match each <u>sentence</u> to its most likely <u>final punctuation</u>.

Ouch, that hurt

Where are we

Who is that

Kai took a photo

Meg asks for help

Wow, yes please

Oh no, look out

Is it raining

3 Put a tick next to the sentences that use <u>sentence punctuation</u> <u>correctly</u> and put a cross next to the ones that <u>don't</u>.

I saw a magician at the circus?

I never said that!

What did you do in Scotland?

What? does Zadie like to eat!

What game did Dylan buy.

Section 7 — Sentence Punctuation © CGP — not to be photocopied

4 **Add the <u>missing punctuation</u> in the boxes below to complete the passage.**

Izzy was doing tricks on her bike.

"Watch this ☐ " she shouted to Charlie.

"What are you doing ☐ " Charlie asked.

"You'll see!" she replied ☐

She jumped ☐ The bike flew through the air like a bird.

"That's amazing ☐ " Charlie cried out.

Use these
punctuation marks:
! . ?

5 **Write a sentence about each of the <u>pictures</u> below ending with the type of <u>punctuation</u> shown beside it.**

➕ (!) ....
....

➕ (.) ....
....

➕ (?) ....
....

"I can punctuate sentences correctly."

Section 8 — Commas

Commas in Lists

Use commas to separate items in a list. There should be a comma between each thing in a list except the last two. These two are separated with 'and' or 'or'.

> I bought a clock, three cushions, two CDs and a book.

1 **Tick the sentences below that use <u>commas</u> correctly.**

I can't eat peanuts, almonds or hazelnuts. ☐

My new trousers are blue, purple, orange and pink. ☐

Steve's cats are called Tiger, Arnold and Mr Fluffs. ☐

I made a cheese tomato and lettuce sandwich. ☐

Dana said she was bored tired and hungry. ☐

My dad plays the guitar, the violin and the flute. ☐

2 **Add <u>commas</u> in the correct places in these sentences.**

I add raspberries blueberries and grapes to my yoghurt.

I can't find my pencil my rubber or my highlighter.

My dog my cat my parrot and my fish all get along very well.

The thieves stole two forks a plate some butter and my duvet.

"I can use commas to separate items in a list."

Commas to Avoid Confusion

You can use commas to make the meaning of a sentence clearer.

> Sam the chef and Katie went home.

This sentence suggests that a chef called Sam and a girl called Katie went home.

> Sam, the chef and Katie went home.

Now it suggests that three people (Sam, Katie and the chef) went home.

1 Add a __comma__ to each sentence below to avoid confusion.

When can we eat Alexander?

I don't like fighting spiders or bananas.

Anaya loves painting elephants and hockey.

Our Christmas involves mince pies singing carols and presents.

2 Read the __two sentences__ below. __Explain__ how the comma __changes__ the meaning of the __second__ sentence.

I helped Mary Taylor and Maneet find the hidden treasure.

I helped Mary, Taylor and Maneet find the hidden treasure.

....

....

....

"I can use commas to avoid confusion."

Commas After Subordinate Clauses

You need to put a **comma** after a **subordinate clause** when it comes at the **beginning** of a sentence:

See pages 14-15 for more on clauses.

When I exercise, my face goes red. ← The main clause makes sense on its own.

You **don't** need a comma if the **subordinate clause comes** after the main clause:

My face goes red when I exercise. ← A subordinate clause doesn't make sense on it's own.

---

1 **Tick the sentences that use <u>commas</u> correctly.**

I made breakfast for my parents, before they went to work. ☐

As the lions slept, the zebras ran away. ☐

There's going to be a heatwave, while we're in Scotland. ☐

While the cake was baking, we made the icing. ☐

---

2 **Underline the <u>subordinate clause</u> in each sentence and add <u>commas</u> where needed.**

When you come round later we could watch a film.

I will tell the truth even if I get in trouble.

She wasn't listening while I explained the instructions.

Since I was in Newcastle I went to see the Angel of the North.

"I can use commas after subordinate clauses."

Commas After Introductions

Adverbial phrases tell you where, when, how or how often something happens.
Use a comma after an adverbial phrase at the beginning of a sentence.

Every morning, I eat fruit for breakfast.

adverbial phrase   comma

1 Add <u>commas</u> in the correct places in the sentences below.

In the future I'd like to learn how to fix cars.

Earlier this week I went to visit my nephew.

As quietly as she could Mary left the room.

In the rainforest you can find lots of different animals.

On Sunday evening we cooked a delicious roast dinner.

2 Rewrite these sentences with <u>commas</u> in the correct places.

At the weekend I like to go walking in the hills.

....

In Brazil there is a big festival called Carnival.

....

On Thursdays I play hockey after school.

....

"I can use commas after adverbial introductions."

Section 8 — Commas

Commas for Extra Information

Use commas to separate extra information in a sentence.

My sister, who is very fit, ran a marathon.

The sentence should still make sense when the extra information is removed.

My sister ran a marathon.

1 Underline the extra information in the sentences below.

Hamsters, which are a type of rodent, are very friendly.

The basket, which was full of eggs, fell on the floor.

Sam, who is my cousin, passed his piano exam.

The museum, which was built in 1904, is still very popular.

We bumped into Kim, our tennis coach, at the supermarket.

Everest, the highest mountain in the world, is very difficult to climb.

2 Put a tick next to the sentences which use commas correctly.

My best friend who is called Aileen, lives next door to me. ☐

The milkman, who works on Mondays, is very friendly. ☐

The café, which serves delicious food, won an award. ☐

I ate, two croissants filled with cheese and eggs, for lunch. ☐

Ceara's grandma, who is very kind, made us all dinner. ☐

(3) **Add <u>commas</u> in the correct places in the sentences below.**

We saw some penguins my favourite animal at the zoo.

Alana's house which is next door to mine has a swimming pool.

My friend who is from Belgium speaks French and German.

The Amazon river found in South America is over 4,000 miles long.

I am going to York where my grandparents live for the weekend.

Big Ben which is in London is a famous building.

Your cousin who is a policeman is coming into school.

(4) **Rewrite these sentences with <u>commas</u> in the correct places.**

The apple which had fallen from the tree was bruised.

....

....

Our tent which is very old has holes in the top.

....

....

The sandwich which I only bought yesterday is already mouldy.

....

....

"I can use commas to separate extra information."

Section 8 — Commas

Comma Practice

Use commas: **for** lists   I swim, run and cycle.

         to avoid confusion   I would like to walk, Michael.

         after an adverbial phrase   Last year, I broke my leg.

         for extra information   Ben, my uncle, is very strong.

1   Match each sentence to the correct <u>reason</u> for using <u>commas</u>.

You need to
shave, Max.

At the start, we all sat in a
circle and said our names.

Olivia, who is a singer,
loves performing on stage.

Gorillas, leopards, monkeys
and snakes live in the jungle.

> separating
> items in a list

> to avoid confusion

> after an
> adverbial phrase

> to add extra
> information

2   Add a <u>comma</u> to each sentence so that it has
the same meaning as the sentence in the box.

After hugging Ted, James
and Melissa left the party.   →   Ted, James and Melissa
are all leaving the party.

Shall we draw Kitty?   →   I am asking Kitty if
she wants to draw.

3 **Put a tick next to the sentences which use <u>commas</u> correctly.**

Zach, who walked 5 miles on Sunday was very tired. ☐

A year ago, today I started playing basketball. ☐

I went to the cinema with Esme, David and Regina. ☐

You have to pay extra for cheese, sauces, and drinks. ☐

The old building, which had been abandoned, was unsafe. ☐

Next winter, I am going skiing with my family. ☐

4 **Circle the <u>comma</u> that isn't needed in each sentence below.**

The suitcase, was very heavy, so I struggled to carry it.

We went to the bank, the post office, and the bakery.

My shoelaces got tangled, together, and I fell over.

Next summer, I'd like to go camping, with my friends.

Christmas Island, near Australia, is home, to millions of red crabs.

5 **Underline the <u>subordinate clauses</u> in each sentence and add <u>commas</u> where needed.**

When I go on holiday I like to play on the beach.

Before you answer the questions read the instructions carefully.

As I left the building I saw my mum waiting.

"I can use commas correctly."

Brackets for Extra Information

A pair of brackets separate extra information in a sentence.

Claude (my oldest cat) scratched Lisa's arm.

The brackets go around the extra information.

The rest of the sentence would still make sense without the extra information.

1 Each sentence below has a <u>bracket</u> in the <u>wrong place</u>.
Cross out this bracket and write a new bracket in the <u>right place</u>.

Mr Mysterious (a famous magician performed) an incredible trick.

The bus driver (a cheerful, elderly) man chatted to the children.

Heidi the hamster (the class pet escaped from) her cage.

Victor's (shoes a pair of trainers) were chewed by the dog.

I found it (the stolen chocolate) bar in Tammy's room.

2 Add <u>brackets</u> to the sentences below in the <u>correct</u> positions.

I saw her the school bully shouting at the boys.

Franco's Place my favourite restaurant is always busy.

The teacher's car an orange one was parked on the street.

Emily's aunt a television presenter came to our school.

The book a travel guide is on the top shelf.

"I can use brackets to show extra informaton."

Dashes for Extra Information

A pair of dashes can separate information in the same way as a pair of brackets.

> Danilo's sister — a talented gymnast — won the competition.

1 **Tick the sentences that use <u>dashes</u> correctly.**

The toad — brown and warty — sat on the rock. ☐

Hugo — my tortoise loves — to eat cabbage. ☐

I dropped the vase — the tall purple — one on the floor. ☐

The pirate — the ship's captain — shouted at the crew. ☐

2 **Each of these sentences needs a <u>pair of dashes</u>.
Put them into the <u>correct</u> boxes.**

Nobody ☐ not even Martin ☐ could solve ☐ the puzzle.

The chicks ☐ cold ☐ and helpless ☐ huddled together.

The houses ☐ the new ones next to ☐ the river ☐ were flooded.

3 **Rewrite the sentence in the <u>correct order</u> using a <u>pair of dashes</u>.**

> won the award   the actor   an Australian

....

"I can use a pair of dashes to show extra information."

Single Dashes

A single dash **can be used to separate** two main clauses.

I opened the book — some of the pages were missing.

The dash creates a pause in the middle of the sentence.

---

1 **Tick the sentences that have used a dash correctly.**

The cat ran across the lawn — the birds flew away. ☐

Abed stacked the books — on the shelf. ☐

The sun shone brightly — it was a beautiful day. ☐

Iona tripped over the branch — she hit the floor hard. ☐

I opened the window — because I was too hot. ☐

Everything had frozen — during the night. ☐

---

2 **Only one of the dashes is needed in each of these sentences.**
Cross out all of the dashes that aren't needed.

The school bell rang — it was time — to go home.

Smoke poured out — of the kitchen — something was burning.

Eliza looked — out of the window — it was snowing heavily.

I paused the film — I could hear something — upstairs.

The teacher — spilled his tea — the children laughed.

"I know how to join two clauses using a single dash."

Hyphens

Hyphens are used to show which word an adjective describes.

| an orange-scented pen | an orange scented pen |

This is a pen that smells of oranges.   This is a 'scented pen' that's orange.

Some words are written with a hyphen so they aren't confused with similar words. For example, words with a prefix.

He re-sorted the socks.   ➡️ This means that he sorted the socks again.

He resorted to shouting.   ➡️ This means that he decided to shout.

---

1 Add a <u>hyphen</u> to each of these sentences so that they match the boxes on the right.

She hates high ☐ heeled ☐ shoes.   ➡️ (shoes with high heels)

The red ☐ winged ☐ insect flew away. ➡️ (an insect with red wings)

That is a short ☐ clawed ☐ lizard.   ➡️ (a lizard with short claws)

I have lots of long ☐ sleeved ☐ shirts. ➡️ (shirts with long sleeves)

---

2 Circle the <u>correct word</u> to complete the sentences so that they make sense.

My cat <u>recovered</u> / <u>re-covered</u> quickly after her operation.

The teacher had to <u>re-mark</u> / <u>remark</u> the children's tests.

"I know what hyphens are and how to use them."

Section 9 — Brackets and Dashes

Section 10 — Apostrophes

Apostrophes for Missing Letters

Use an **apostrophe** to show where **you've** left letters out of a **shortened word**.

I will ➡ I'll   you have ➡ you've   will not ➡ won't

Sometimes the shortened word **doesn't** quite match the words **it's** made from.

1 Complete the sentences using the <u>shortened form</u> of the words in the boxes.

should have ➡ You ....should've............ answered your phone.

could not ➡ Kirsty .... come today.

you would ➡ .... like the view from the hills.

you are ➡ .... late because you overslept.

I am ➡ Do you think .... funny?

2 Rewrite the <u>longer version</u> of the underlined word in the box below.

<u>How's</u> the weather today?

| How is |

<u>They'll</u> know what to do.

| |

She <u>could've</u> asked for help.

| |

He <u>hadn't</u> found his wallet.

| |

<u>I'd</u> forgotten his name.

| |

Seb <u>didn't</u> like chopping onions.

| |

"I can use apostrophes for missing letters."

Section 10 — Apostrophes   *© CGP — not to be photocopied*

Its and It's

The words 'its' and 'it's' mean two **different** things.

its This means 'belonging to it'. ⟹ the dog wags its tail

it's This means 'it is' or 'it has'. ⟹ it's hot   it's fallen over

1 Tick the sentences which use '<u>its</u>' or '<u>it's</u>' correctly.

The lion shook it's mane as it rose. ☐

It's been a lovely afternoon at the beach. ☐

The shop opened its doors at nine o'clock. ☐

The game was in it's final minute. ☐

I think that its for the best if we go now. ☐

2 Write '<u>its</u>' or '<u>it's</u>' to complete the <u>sentences</u> below.

I don't think that .... a big problem.

A spider catches flies in .... web.

.... been snowing in the mountains.

Dad's car has a lot of space in .... boot.

.... taken a long time to get here.

.... great to see you!

"I can use the words 'its' and 'it's' correctly."

Apostrophes for Possession

You can use apostrophes to show that someone or something owns something.

For singular nouns, and plural ➡ the alien's ship   the octopus's dinner
nouns that don't end in 's',
add an apostrophe and 's'. ➡ the children's toys

If a plural noun ends in 's', you only add the apostrophe. ➡ the cats' toys

1 Complete these phrases by writing out the word in the box to show <u>possession</u>.

shop ➡ the ...shop's... sale   Jo ➡ .... hamster

school ➡ my .... field   bus ➡ the .... bell

girl ➡ the .... ball   Rome ➡ .... ruins

2 Rewrite each phrase so that it changes from <u>singular</u> to <u>plural</u>.

<u>singular</u>	<u>plural</u>
the teacher's instructions	the teachers' instructions
the car's wheels	
the song's words	
the game's rules	
the class's pens	
the cake's candles	

"I can use apostrophes to show possession."

Apostrophe Practice

You can use apostrophes to show where letters are missing, or to show possession for nouns. Remember that 'its' and 'it's' are two different words.

(1) Put a cross next to the sentences which use <u>apostrophes</u> incorrectly. Write out the <u>shortened form</u> using an <u>apostrophe</u> correctly.

Lets' go to the beach today. ☐ ....

The dog didn't bite Fergus. ☐ ....

Your'e going to come with us. ☐ ....

I wou'ldve liked to visit the zoo. ☐ ....

We'd like to see you again soon. ☐ ....

Theyd' been to visit Anais. ☐ ....

(2) Add <u>apostrophes</u> to the underlined words below to show possession.

My <u>m u m s</u> name is Karina and she works in an office.

We ate at <u>P a r i s s</u> most popular restaurant.

The <u>h o u s e s</u> garden was wild and full of weeds.

A guide told the <u>m u s e u m s</u> visitors to be quiet.

(3) Write a sentence about the picture using the word '<u>its</u>' correctly.

....

"I can use apostrophes correctly."

Section 10 — Apostrophes

Section 11 — Inverted Commas

Punctuating Speech

Speech always ends with a **punctuation** mark, which goes **inside** the speech marks.

Nigel said, "Follow me."

capital letter

Speech marks are also called inverted commas.

If speech starts **part-way** through the **sentence**, you need a **comma before** the speech. ⟶ Nigel said, "Follow me."

If the speech is **continued**, you **don't need** to start with a **capital letter**.

"I think," he said, "you should follow me."

lower case

---

1 Tick the sentences which are **punctuated correctly**.

Everyone shouted, "Get on with the show" ☐

"I want beans on toast for breakfast," said Camille. ☐

"I can't believe he did that" said Tariq. ☐

"Who here," said the teacher, "has done the homework?" ☐

---

2 Circle the **punctuation mistake** in each sentence, then draw a line to the **correct book**.

Paolo asked, "when will dinner be ready?"

"I never make mistakes" said Professor Stirling.

"Before you go," said Trisha, "you must meet him".

"This is utterly disgraceful"! shouted Freda.

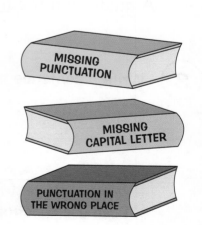

MISSING PUNCTUATION

MISSING CAPITAL LETTER

PUNCTUATION IN THE WRONG PLACE

---

3 Put <u>inverted commas</u> (speech marks) in the <u>correct places</u> in the sentences below.

Turn the music down ! shouted Jodi's neighbour .

George asked , What should I do about it ?

Let's go to the beach , said Eve , because it's a lovely day .

Give me the car keys , said Sandrine , as I'm late for work .

4 Add the <u>correct punctuation</u> to the boxes below to complete each sentence.

Darcy shouted ☐ "Leave me alone ☐ "

☐ I want to see Buckingham Palace ☐ " said Lin.

"Who wants to watch a film tonight ☐ " asked Peter ☐

"The problem is," said Humphrey ☐ "we don't know where it is. ☐

Mason said, ☐ I don't like broccoli, but I love biscuits ☐ "

5 Rewrite each sentence using <u>inverted commas</u> and the <u>correct punctuation</u>.

When are we going to set off asked Rupert

....

Here are the results of the experiment announced Kyle

....

"I can punctuate speech correctly." 👍✓ 🤏✓ 👎✓

Section 11 — Inverted Commas

Direct and Reported Speech

You only use speech marks if you're writing down exactly what someone has said. This is called direct speech.

> "I'm going to Ireland," said Steph.

⟵ This is direct speech — it's exactly what Steph has said.

If you're just talking about what someone has said, you don't need speech marks. This is called reported speech.

> Steph said that she's going to Ireland.

⟵ This is reported speech — it's just reporting what she said.

1 Draw lines to show whether each of these sentences is <u>direct speech</u> or <u>reported speech</u>.

They said they would be here.

"I don't understand," said Terry.

"Can you pass me the salt?" asked Greta.

He told me you wanted to leave.

Yuri yelled, "Listen to me!"

I heard Michal say he likes jazz music.

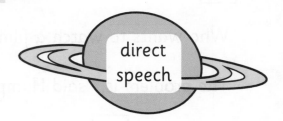

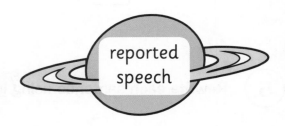

2 Tick the sentences which need <u>inverted commas</u>.

My sister told me she wants to see that film. ☐

I bought you flowers, said Gary, and some chocolates. ☐

What a beautiful gift! said Marie. ☐

Rita and Elijah say I need singing lessons. ☐

3 Write the sentences on the whiteboard to show whether they are <u>direct speech</u> or <u>reported speech</u>.

"My pigs have escaped!"

He asked for directions.

They talked about the film.

"When does it open?"

"I went to the museum."

She said she was tired.

Direct speech	Reported speech
....	....
....	....
....	....

4 Add <u>inverted commas</u> to the sentences that <u>need them</u>. If a sentence is already punctuated <u>correctly</u>, put a <u>tick</u> in the box.

Lucas said he's going swimming this weekend . ☐

Don't forget to water all the plants , said Mum . ☐

My best friend says we can go with them tomorrow . ☐

Neil told me it was closed , but I don't believe him . ☐

Nobody move , whispered the explorer , and keep quiet . ☐

I like painting , I heard him say . ☐

She had asked to play outside , but she wasn't allowed . ☐

"I can use direct speech and reported speech."

Section 11 — Inverted Commas

Colons

Colons can be used to introduce a list or an explanation.

> Dad had several things to buy: bread, milk, bananas and cheese.

In an explanation, the first part is explained by the second part.

> I'm so happy: it's my birthday.

The part before the colon must always be a main clause.

---

1 **Tick the sentences which use colons correctly.**

Isra likes reading comics, baking: and riding horses. ☐

Tyrese has three best friends: Asher, Talisha and Lee. ☐

You have a choice of ice cream: vanilla: mint: or: chocolate. ☐

I enjoy the creative subjects: music, art, dance and drama. ☐

I want: to watch: a cartoon, musical or action film. ☐

---

2 **Write a list of the items in the pictures to complete the sentences below. Use a colon to introduce your list.**

Hari picks his outfit ....

....

....

I packed my favourite things ....

....

....

3 These sentences have <u>too many colons</u>. Circle the <u>colons</u> which are <u>not</u> needed.

I can't buy: that beautiful necklace: it's too expensive.

Rosa went home at 5 o'clock: she needed: to be back: before dark.

Alan: laughed at Oskar's joke: Oskar told the best jokes.

Tell Susi: that I'll be late: the train: hasn't arrived yet.

4 Add a <u>colon</u> to the correct place in each sentence.

I am going to put on suncream it's really sunny.

Tegan gave her green sweets to me she hates them.

Rupert does know Riley they're cousins.

I'll go to the shop tomorrow it's getting late now.

5 Use a <u>colon</u> to join each pair of clauses into a single sentence.

I hope it's lunchtime soon ➕ (:) ➕ I'm hungry

....

I love the monkey bars ➕ (:) ➕ I'm really good at them

....

We have to go to school ➕ (:) ➕ it's Monday

....

"I can use colons to introduce lists and explanations."

Section 12 — Colons and Semi-Colons

Semi-Colons

Semi-colons **can separate** long phrases **or** clauses **in a** list.
This is usually when there are other punctuation marks **in the items.**

> I ordered two hamburgers, one without sauce; three small, plain portions of chips; and some chicken nuggets.

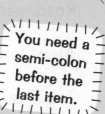

You need a semi-colon before the last item.

Semi-colons **can also** join two clauses **in a sentence. They both have to be** main clauses, equally important **and** about the same thing.

> Tessa hated the show; Thomas thought it was great.

1 Tick the sentences which use <u>semi-colons</u> correctly.

My bike is yellow; my sister's bike is green. ☐

Christmas cake is fruit cake because; it's traditional. ☐

Dad is thirty-nine; Uncle George is forty-one. ☐

I like; chocolate apples are good for you. ☐

Simon likes playing snap; Lily prefers chess. ☐

2 Join these main clauses with <u>semi-colons</u> to make a single sentence.

Anya walks to school   Liam gets the bus

....

Syed likes strawberries   Lacey likes plums

....

3 Add the missing <u>semi-colons</u> to these lists.

I own one lazy, old dog called Rascal two kittens, which I got from the shelter and a rabbit with floppy ears.

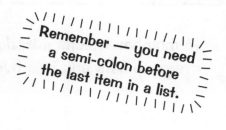
Remember — you need a semi-colon before the last item in a list.

School dinner was either pepperoni pizza and potato wedges a jacket potato with beans, which was the vegetarian option or a hot, spicy chilli.

The painter painted a castle, which was in ruins some tall, snowy mountains and a dark green forest in moonlight.

4 Finish the sentence below using the <u>words</u> in the puzzle pieces and <u>semi-colons</u>.

six cupcakes, which had cherries on top

three delicious, crunchy chocolate chip cookies

and one whole apple pie

At the school bake sale, Zak sold ....

....

....

....

"I can break up lists and sentences with semi-colons."

Colons and Semi-Colons Practice

Remember, colons introduce lists and explanations, and semi-colons break up lists and join two equally important main clauses in a sentence.

1 Add the <u>punctuation</u> into each sentence in the correct place.

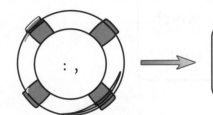

There are three choices of pizza cheese pepperoni or mushroom.

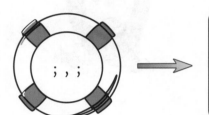

At the campsite, I set up the three-person tent I started a fire which took a while and I roasted some marshmallows.

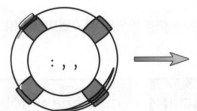

My cat had four kittens Tiger Bella Ginger and Socks.

2 Draw lines connecting the statements most likely to be joined with a <u>colon</u>.

Sasha played inside

I ran 10 miles this week

Kobi won the game

We must buy a ticket today

I'm preparing for a marathon.

he rolled a six.

the show will sell out quickly.

it was raining.

3 Write out the <u>words</u> and <u>punctuation</u> in the crates into <u>full sentences</u>.

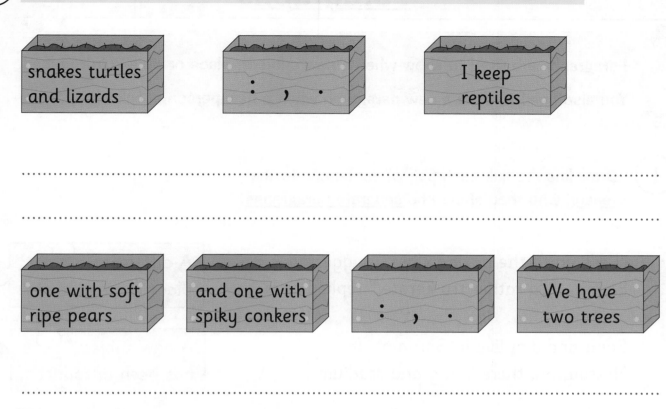

snakes turtles and lizards

: , .

I keep reptiles

....

....

one with soft ripe pears

and one with spiky conkers

: , .

We have two trees

....

....

4 Add a <u>semi-colon</u> into each sentence in the correct place.

On Tuesdays, I play squash on Fridays, I play tennis.

Charlotte likes peas she doesn't like sweetcorn.

Talia plays the clarinet Shane plays the flute.

This flight is to Japan that one is to Australia.

Clocks go forward in spring they go back in autumn.

Elliot got six questions right Matt got four questions right.

"I can use colons and semi-colons correctly."

Section 12 — Colons and Semi-Colons

Section 13 — Paragraphs and Layout

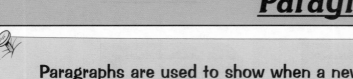

Paragraphs

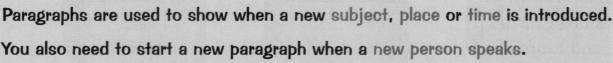

Paragraphs are used to show when a new subject, place or time is introduced.

You also need to start a new paragraph when a new person speaks.

1 Draw lines to link each pair of sentences to the reason why they should be separate paragraphs.

"Let's go to the boxing class," suggested Emma. "I'd rather try karate," replied Sam.

Sona and Jim live in Barnam. In Nessington, there is a grand stadium.

The team met for practice at 10 am. At 3 pm, the tournament began.

The children are starting to settle down. My cat hasn't been very well recently.

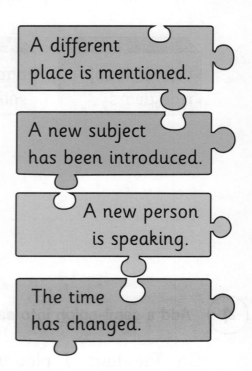

A different place is mentioned.

A new subject has been introduced.

A new person is speaking.

The time has changed.

2 Write a sentence that could go in the same paragraph as the sentences below.

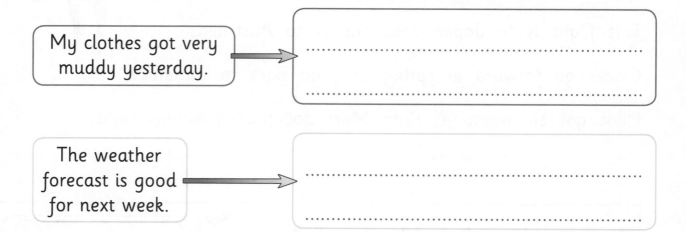

My clothes got very muddy yesterday.

....

....

The weather forecast is good for next week.

....

....

3 Add <u>four</u> paragraph markers (//) to the passage to show where new <u>paragraphs</u> should start.

We were heading inside for the night when we heard a noise coming from the end of the garden. "Take your sister inside," said Dad, already moving towards the noise. "But Dad, I want to come with you!" I protested. "It's probably just a bird. If it's exciting I'll call you, I promise," he said, smiling, as he strolled down the path towards the bushes. As we got to the door, I heard Dad shout, "Girls, come quickly! You need to see this!"

4 Read the passage below, then circle the correct <u>reason</u> for each <u>new paragraph</u>.

"I don't understand how they've managed to escape," Sian said, as she checked all the fences in the field.

Her boss called the donkeys, hoping to lure them back to the farm. He didn't like it when they wandered off into the countryside.

Last month, the donkeys had escaped for the first time. Sian was sure she always locked the gate when she left work...

"They'll come back eventually," said her boss reassuringly.

2nd paragraph ⟹ new subject / change of time

3rd paragraph ⟹ change of time / change of place

4th paragraph ⟹ change of place / new person speaking

"I can organise a piece of writing into paragraphs."

Layout Devices

There are lots of different **layout devices** that help to make the **presentation of** informative writing **more interesting:**

| headings | subheadings | bullet points | boxes | tables |

1 Label the different <u>layout features</u> in the poster below.

1. ....

2. ....

3. ....

4. ....

5. ....

"I can identify layout features."

Writing Lists

You can use numbered points or bullet points to write a list.
Always introduce a list with a colon.

Road safety:
1) Always use crossings.
2) Look both ways.
3) Listen for approaching cars.

Shopping list:
· Yoghurt,
· Bread rolls,
· Tissues.

If you use a capital letter at the start of one point, use capitals at the start of all the points.

You can also use commas or semi-colons at the end of each bullet point, with a full stop after the final point.

1 Complete the list of <u>bullet points</u> using words from the passage.

To be a good friend, you should be considerate of other people's feelings. You need to be trustworthy and you should always be honest. It's also important to be a good listener.

Qualities of a good friend:

· considerate

....

....

....

....

2 Complete the <u>numbered list</u> with <u>three</u> more things you do in the morning.

In the morning, I:

1) have a drink of water

....

....

....

"I can organise information into lists."

Section 14 — Prefixes

Prefixes — 'under' 'over' 'en' and 'em'

A prefix is a letter or group of letters that can be added to the beginning of a word (called a root word) to make a new word.

prefix → over ➕ root word ↗ rated → overrated

The spelling of the root word does not change when a prefix is added.

1 Add <u>over</u>- or <u>under</u>- to the sentences below so that they make sense.

Let's find a cheaper vase — this one is .... priced.

My broccoli turned to mush because it was .... cooked.

Don't .... estimate her abilities — she's very clever.

If I .... eat, I feel too full and get a stomach ache.

My friends don't like it, but I think the film is .... appreciated.

Shauni is very tired because she is .... worked.

2 Use the clues to work out each word beginning with <u>en</u>- or <u>em</u>-.

to hire ➡ [ ][ ][p][l][o][y]

[ ][ ][r][a][g][e] ⬅ make angry

make possible ➡ [ ][ ][a][ ][l][e]

[ ][ ][b][r][a][ ][e] ⬅ hug

put a spell on ➡ [ ][ ][c][ ][a][n][t]

Prefixes — 'mid' 'pre' 'fore' and 'non'

Prefixes can give us useful information about a root word.

'mid-' means 'middle'.   'pre-' and 'fore-' mean 'before'.   'non-' means 'not'.

| midway | preheat | forewarn | nonliving |

1 Draw lines to match each word to the **correct prefix**.
Then write the completed words on the **board**.

 mid

 pre

 fore

 non

ground

air

sense

view

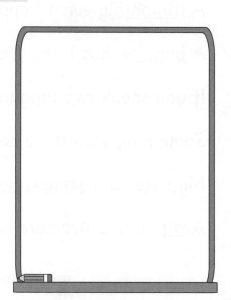

2 Complete the words in these sentences using **mid-**, **pre-**, **fore-** or **non-**.

I always have a cup of tea and a slice of cake at .... day.

The weather .... cast is good for this weekend.

The bread didn't take long to cook because it was .... baked.

The dog had been barking .... stop all day.

My .... head hurts because I banged it when I fell over.

They reached the .... point in their journey.

Prefixes — 'bi' 'tri' and 'semi'

Prefixes can give us useful information about a root word.

| 'bi' means 'two'. | 'tri' means 'three'. | 'semi' means 'half' or 'partly'. |

1 Tick the sentences where the underlined word has the **correct prefix**.

A <u>trimonthly</u> event happens three times a month. ☐

A <u>biathlon</u> has three events in it. ☐

If you speak two languages, you are <u>trilingual</u>. ☐

Something with three colours is <u>tricolour</u>. ☐

My sister is a <u>semiprofessional</u> athlete. ☐

A <u>tripod</u> is a structure with three legs. ☐

2 Unscramble the words in the boxes. They all start with <u>bi-</u>, <u>tri-</u> or <u>semi-</u>. Use the <u>definitions</u> on the right to help you.

The first and last letters are in the correct places.

s m f e i n i a l	....	the round before the final
t c i y r l c e	....	a bike with three wheels
s i r m d e y	....	partly dry
t p i r r a t	....	something with three parts
b w e i e l k y	....	twice a week

3 Use the picture clues to <u>work out</u> what each word is. Write the words in the boxes.

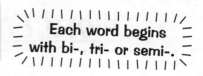

Each word begins with bi-, tri- or semi-.

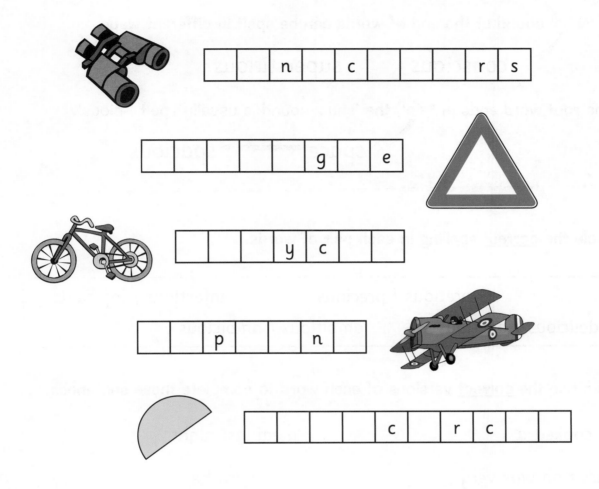

| | | n | | c | | | | r | s |

| | | | | | g | | e |

| | | | y | c | |

| | | p | | | n | |

| | | | | c | | r | c | |

4 Replace each <u>underlined</u> word with one that has the correct prefix.

I live in a <u>bidetached</u> house.

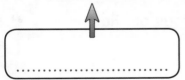

The <u>triannual</u> trip happens twice a year.

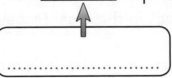

They moved to a <u>trirural</u> town.

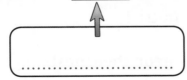

My mum is now <u>biretired</u>.

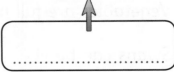

Word Endings — the 'shus' sound

The 'shus' sound at the end of words can be spelt in different ways.

conscious   **superstitious**

If the root word ends in '-ce', the 'shus' sound is usually spelt '-cious'.

space → **spacious**

1 Circle the <u>correct</u> spelling in each pair of words.

> pretious / precious   infectious / infecious
>
> delicious / delitious   ambitious / ambicious

Then use the <u>correct</u> versions of each word to complete these sentences.

Eva cooked a .... meal last night.

Mila's ring was very .... to her.

The builders had .... plans for the garden.

I picked up an .... disease on holiday.

2 Complete the words in these sentences using -<u>cious</u> or -<u>tious</u>.

My cat is quite gentle — she isn't mali................... .

The characters in the book aren't real — they are ficti................... .

Vegetables are full of vitamins — they're nutri................... .

Swans can be vi................... if you go near their nest.

I think black cats bring bad luck — I am supersti................... .

3 Draw lines from the <u>word beginnings</u> to the correct <u>word endings</u>.

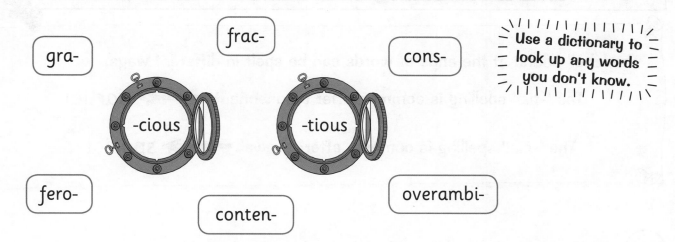

gra-

frac-

cons-

-cious

-tious

fero-

conten-

overambi-

Use a dictionary to look up any words you don't know.

4 Circle the <u>correct</u> spelling of each word to complete the sentences below.

The restaurant's food was absolutely <u>atrocious</u> / <u>atrotious</u>.

I didn't want to sound <u>ungracious</u> / <u>ungratious</u>.

The apple pie was utterly <u>scrumpcious</u> / <u>scrumptious</u>.

There had been plenty of rain, so the grass was <u>lutious</u> / <u>luscious</u>.

The police found a <u>suspitious</u> / <u>suspicious</u> car in the woods.

The doctor helped the woman who was <u>unconscious</u> / <u>unconstious</u>.

5 Write a <u>sentence</u> using each of the following words.

cautious

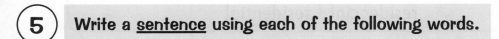

spacious

Word Endings — the 'shul' sound

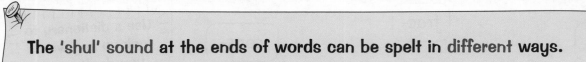

The 'shul' sound at the ends of words can be spelt in different ways.

The '-tial' spelling is common after a consonant. ⟹ par**tial**

The '-cial' spelling is common after a vowel. ⟹ spa**cial**

1 Write the **correct** spelling of each word on the dotted lines.

crucial / crutial ⟹ ....

ratial / racial ⟹ ....

confidencial / confidential ⟹ ....

facial / fatial ⟹ ....

2 Circle the **correct** spelling in each pair of words.

torrential / torrencial   benefitial / beneficial

marcial / martial   residencial / residential

Then use the **correct** versions of each word to complete these sentences.

We got soaked in the .... rain.

They live on a quiet .... estate.

My older sister takes .... art classes.

Running is very .... for your health.

3 Circle the <u>correct spelling</u> of each word to complete the sentence.

The criminal stole their <u>financial</u> / <u>finantial</u> information.

The police received reports of <u>antisotial</u> / <u>antisocial</u> behaviour.

David's first <u>initial</u> / <u>inicial</u> is 'D'.

Cole has the <u>potencial</u> / <u>potential</u> to be a great baseball player.

Auntie Sue gave me <u>imparcial</u> / <u>impartial</u> advice on my problem.

4 Rearrange the letters below to complete the words ending in -<u>tial</u> or -<u>cial</u>.

| o | | f | | | | l |

| e | s | | n | | a | |

| | | o | | i | |

5 Tick the words that are spelt <u>correctly</u>.
Then use each correct word in a <u>sentence</u>.

special ☐   spetial ☐

....

artifitial ☐   artificial ☐

....

Word Endings — 'ant' and 'ent'

Sometimes words ending in '-ant' or '-ent' sound similar, but are spelt differently.

elegant   evident

Both the '-ant' and '-ent' endings sound like '-unt'.

1 Draw lines to match each word beginning to the <u>correct ending</u>. Then write the completed words on the <u>board</u>.

sil-

dec-

dist-

pati-

mut-

brilli-

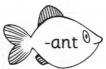

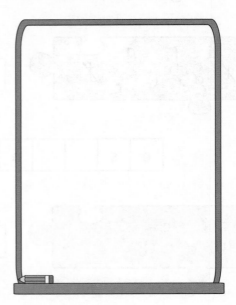

2 Circle the <u>correct</u> spelling of each word to complete the sentences below.

The explorers made a <u>significant</u> / <u>significent</u> discovery.

My work is <u>consistent</u> / <u>consistant</u>, so my teachers are pleased.

I'm learning a new dance for the school <u>talant</u> / <u>talent</u> show.

There was an <u>incident</u> / <u>incidant</u> at school today.

I wasn't sure, so I was <u>hesitant</u> / <u>hesitent</u> to put my hand up.

3 Rearrange the letters below to complete the words ending in -<u>ant</u> or -<u>ent</u>.

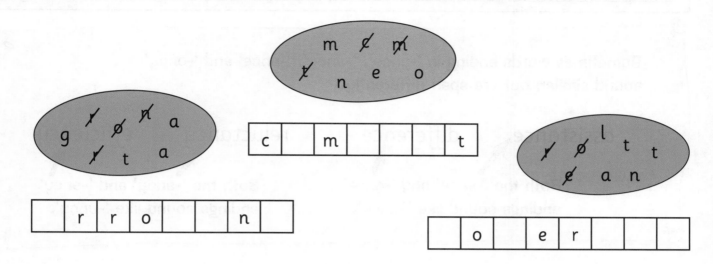

| c | m | | | | t |

| | r | r | o | | | n | |

| | | o | | e | r | | | |

4 Add -<u>ant</u> or -<u>ent</u> to complete the words below.
Then write the words out in full.

eleph- **+** .... ➡ ....

presid- **+** .... ➡ ....

differ- **+** .... ➡ ....

assist- **+** .... ➡ ....

5 Complete the words in these sentences using -<u>ant</u> or -<u>ent</u>.

I live on the contin.............. of Europe.

Priya can talk to anyone — she is more confid.............. than me.

I always try to be kind and pleas.............. when I meet new people.

Olly is very intellig.............. — he got full marks in his exams.

Sunita does things for herself because she is independ.............. .

I bought a fragr.............. candle that smells like black cherry.

Word Endings — 'ance', 'ancy' and 'ence', 'ency'

Sometimes words ending in '-ance', '-ancy', '-ence' and '-ency' sound similar, but are spelt differently.

assistance   difference   reluctancy   efficiency

Both the '-ance' and '-ence' endings sound like '-unce'.

Both the '-ancy' and '-ency' endings sound like '-uncy'.

1 Underline the **correct** spelling of each word.

consequence consequance

guidence   guidance

infency   infancy

agancy   agency

decency decancy

resistance   resistence

2 Complete these words using '-**ance**', '-**ancy**', '-**ence**' or '-**ency**'. Use the definitions in brackets to help you.

import .... (the significance of something)

appli .... (a machine or gadget, e.g. a fridge)

expect .... (a feeling that something is going to happen)

obedi .... (doing what you're told)

frequ .... (how often something happens)

3 | Circle the **correct** spelling of each word to complete the sentences below.

The policeman asked to see my driving <u>licence</u> / <u>licance</u>.

Bianca's mum is taking part in an <u>endurance</u> / <u>endurence</u> race.

He has a <u>tendency</u> / <u>tendancy</u> to sleep through his morning alarms.

The <u>attendence</u> / <u>attendance</u> at the football match was fantastic.

She asked me to deliver the parcel as a matter of <u>urgency</u> / <u>urgancy</u>.

The lawyer tried to prove the man's <u>innocance</u> / <u>innocence</u>.

4 | Solve the **clues** to complete the crossword.

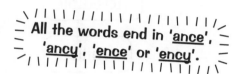
All the words end in '**ance**', '**ancy**', '**ence**' or '**ency**'.

Across

1. Another word for money

2. Belief in yourself

3. To move forward

Down

1. An opening, e.g. for a job

2. Another word for a crisis

3. The nine month period before a baby is born

|

Word Endings — 'able' and 'ible'

Sometimes words ending in '-able' and '-ible' sound similar, but are spelt differently.

breakable   convertible

1 Draw lines to show which spellings are __correct__ and which are __incorrect__.

laughable

incredible

availible

payable

reasonible

Correct spelling

Incorrect spelling

laughible

incredable

available

payible

reasonable

2 Circle the __correct__ spelling of each word to complete the sentences below.

The cake went mouldy, so it was no longer __edible__ / __edable__.

My brother isn't very __likeable__ / __likible__ — he's really mean to me.

Doing gymnastics has made me very __flexible__ / __flexable__.

My best friend is always happy and __excitible__ / __excitable__.

Going to bed early is __preferable__ / __preferible__ to staying up late.

I haven't drunk enough water, so I have a __terrable__ / __terrible__ headache.

Our new sofa is more __comfortible__ / __comfortable__ than our old one.

3 Use the clues to work out each word ending in -<u>able</u> or -<u>ible</u>.

cute ➡ | a | d | o | r | | | |

| p | o | s | s | | | | ⬅ can be done

quite large ➡ | s | i | z | e | | | |

4 Unscramble the words in the boxes. Use the definitions to help you. Each word ends with -<u>able</u> or -<u>ible</u>.

The first and last letters are in the correct places.

v s i b l i e .... can be seen

s t a i b l u e .... appropriate

r v e r e b i l s e .... can be changed back

c p a l b a e .... able to do something

b i e l a v b e l e .... convincing

5 Complete the words in these sentences using -<u>able</u> or -<u>ible</u>.

The most desir.............. chocolates in a box are eaten first.

"You can't beat me," shouted the villain, "I'm invinc..............!"

Stefani likes to wear very fashion.............. clothes.

They threw me a surprise party, and it was really enjoy.............. .

She tried to be quiet, but we could all hear her very aud.............. whisper.

Marc doesn't like celery — he thinks it tastes horr.............. .

Word Endings — 'ably' and 'ibly'

Sometimes words ending in '-ably' and '-ibly' sound similar, but are spelt differently.

reli**ably**   leg**ibly**

Both the '-ably' and '-ibly' endings sound like 'ubly'.

1 Choose -<u>ably</u> or -<u>ibly</u> to add to each <u>word beginning</u> below. Then write the completed word in the <u>correct</u> column.

forc-   admir-   predict-   irrespons-

<u>-ably</u>   <u>-ibly</u>

....

....

2 Read the clues below, then <u>complete</u> the words.

All the words will end in -<u>ably</u> or -<u>ibly</u>.

in a disagreeable way

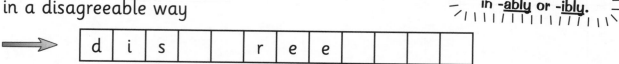
⟹ | d | i | s | | | r | e | e | | | |

in a cross way

⟹ | i | r | r | i | t | | | | | |

in a favourable way

⟹ | f | a | v | o | | r | | | | |

to say something is likely

⟹ | p | r | o | b | | | | |

in a way that can't be resisted

⟹ | i | r | r | e | s | | s | t | | | |

3 Rearrange the letters below to complete the words ending in -<u>ably</u> or -<u>ibly</u>.

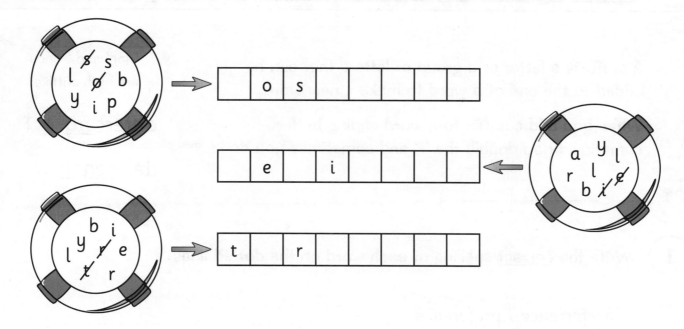

| | o | s | | | | |

| | e | | i | | | |

| t | | r | | | | |

4 Circle the <u>correct</u> spelling of each word to complete the sentences below.

Last Thursday, it was <u>unbearably</u> / <u>unbearibly</u> hot.

The thief, dressed in black, ran <u>invisibly</u> / <u>invisably</u> through the streets.

Karen is mature and always acts <u>responsably</u> / <u>responsibly</u>.

In the video game, the car was spinning <u>uncontrollibly</u> / <u>uncontrollably</u>.

5 Complete the words in these sentences using -<u>ably</u> or -<u>ibly</u>.

The children all behaved sens.............. on the school trip.

The new skyscraper they have built seems imposs.............. tall.

They didn't win, but the girls were argu.............. the best relay team.

Our kitchen is consider.............. more modern than it used to be.

My local rugby team played reason.............. well at the weekend.

Section 15 — Word Endings and Suffixes

Adding Suffixes to Words Ending in 'fer'

A suffix is a letter or a group of letters that can be added to the end of a word to make a new word.

When you add a suffix to a word ending in 'fer', sometimes you double the 'r' and sometimes you don't. ⟶

'-ing' and '-ence' are both suffixes

deferr**ing**

defer**ence**

1 Write the **correct** spelling of each word on the dotted lines.

preferrence / preference

....

referrence / reference

....

indifference / indifferrence

....

2 Circle the **correct** spelling of each word to complete the sentences below. Then write the correct words on the **board**.

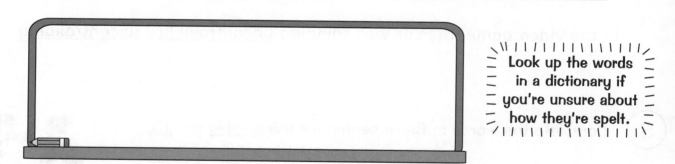

Look up the words in a dictionary if you're unsure about how they're spelt.

Leila was <u>offering</u> / <u>offerring</u> her sweets to the class.

I was <u>referring</u> / <u>refering</u> to my hamster, not my guinea pig.

I chose the window seat, <u>preferring</u> / <u>prefering</u> to look outside.

Toma was <u>sufferring</u> / <u>suffering</u> from a headache.

We had <u>differring</u> / <u>differing</u> opinions on what we wanted to eat.

3 Add the suffix -<u>ence</u> to complete the words below.
Then write the words out in full.

differ- ➕ .... ➡ ....

infer- ➕ .... ➡ ....

confer- ➕ .... ➡ ....

4 Circle the <u>correct</u> spelling in each pair of words.

prefered / preferred   referred / refered
transferred / transfered

Then use the <u>correct</u> versions of each word to complete these sentences.

The vet .... to my cat by the wrong name.

We .... our luggage from the house to the car.

When I was younger, I .... the colour yellow.

5 Tick the words that are spelt <u>correctly</u>.
Then use each correct word in a <u>sentence</u>.

offered ☐   offerred ☐

....

sufferred ☐   suffered ☐

....

Section 15 — Word Endings and Suffixes

Section 16 — Confusing Words

'ei' and 'ie' Words

Use this rhyme to help you remember how to spell ei and ie words:

'i' before 'e' except after 'c' if the vowel sound rhymes with bee

chief ← Rhymes with bee, so 'i' before 'e'.

receipt ← Rhymes with bee but follows a 'c' — so 'e' before 'i'.

foreign ← Doesn't rhyme with bee, so 'e' before 'i'.

science ← Doesn't rhyme with bee but follows a 'c' — so 'i' before 'e'.

1 Add <u>ie</u> or <u>ei</u> to each of the words below.

th .... f   dec .... ve   rec .... ve   p .... ce

2 Put a tick next to the words that are <u>spelt correctly</u> and a cross next to those <u>spelt incorrectly</u>.

shield ☐   cieling ☐

wieght ☐   neighbour ☐

soceity ☐   acheive ☐

3 Complete the words below using either <u>ei</u> or <u>ie</u>.

br .... f   r .... gn   f .... rce

n .... gh   bel .... ve   misch .... f

Some words don't follow the 'i before e' rule. You just have to learn these words.

seize — Rhymes with bee, but is spelt 'ei'.

'neither' and 'either' can be pronounced differently, which confuses the 'rhymes with bee' rule.

neither   either

4 Circle the misspelt words.

wierd   hieght   field

niece   retreive   anceint

5 The ei and ie parts of the words below are missing. Draw lines to match each word to its missing part.

nutr**?**nt   d**?**sel

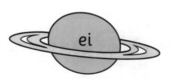
ei

n**?**ther   p**?**r

ie

dec**?**t   **?**ther

6 Circle the correct spelling of each word to complete the sentences below.

Edmund <u>siezed</u> / <u>seized</u> the ball and ran.

My <u>freind</u> / <u>friend</u> is moving to Manchester.

Eggs are good sources of <u>protein</u> / <u>protien</u>.

Tea and coffee are high in <u>caffiene</u> / <u>caffeine</u>.

Section 16 — Confusing Words

Words with 'ough' in

Words that contain the letters 'ough' can sound very different. For example:

Here the 'ough' letters sound like 'oh'.

thought

Here the 'ough' letters sound like 'uh'.

though

Here the 'ough' letters sound like 'or'.

thorough

1   Put a tick in the box next to the <u>ough</u> word that has an '<u>oh</u>' sound.

trough ☐   dough ☐   fought ☐   wrought ☐

2   Draw lines to match each <u>ough</u> word with the correct <u>sound</u>.

brought   bought

'uff'

drought   bough

'ow'

enough   tough

'or'

rough   sought

3   Draw lines to link the pairs of <u>ough</u> words that <u>rhyme</u>.

thorough   though   ought

dough   sought   borough

4 **Solve the clues to find the ough words.**

something you do when you're ill ⟹ | c | | | |

another word for 'zero' ⟹ | n | | | |

the opposite of smooth ⟹ | r | | |

another word for 'argued' ⟹ | f | | | | |

part of a tree ⟹ | b | | | |

another word for 'strong' ⟹ | t | | | |

5 **Fill the gaps in the sentences below using the ough words in the boxes.**

(although)   (through)   (bought)   (ought)   (enough)

Michael .... a souvenir on holiday.

.... I was tired, I worked hard.

The train went .... a tunnel.

I .... to go to sleep early tonight.

There wasn't .... time to score another goal.

6 **Write a sentence using each of the following ough words.**

plough ....

thought ....

Section 16 — Confusing Words

Words with Silent Letters

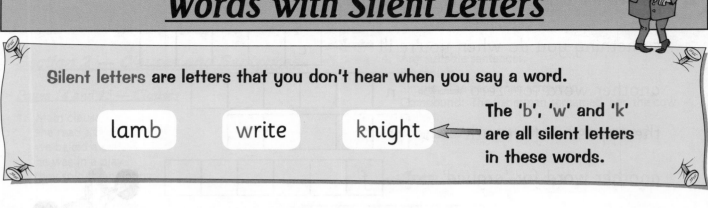

Silent letters are letters that you don't hear when you say a word.

lamb   write   knight ← The 'b', 'w' and 'k' are all silent letters in these words.

1 Circle the silent letters in each of the words below.

p l u m b e r   c a l m   g n a r l e d   s o l e m n

h o u r   l i s t e n   k n e e   i s l a n d

2 For each word below, write the silent letter in the box.

ghost ☐   column ☐   guitar ☐

watch ☐   sign ☐   honest ☐

3 Sort the words below into the correct group based on their silent letter.

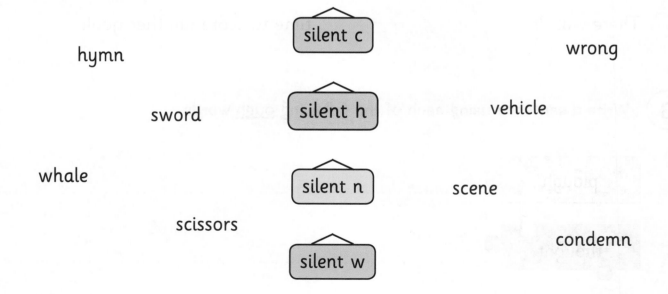

hymn   silent c   wrong

sword   silent h   vehicle

whale   silent n   scene

scissors

silent w   condemn

4 Circle the <u>correct spelling</u> of each word to complete the sentences below.

On his trip to the farm, Rahul saw a cow and its <u>carf</u> / <u>calf</u>.

The dog <u>gnawed</u> / <u>knawed</u> on its rubber bone.

There were some daisies among the <u>thistles</u> / <u>thissles</u>.

The goat <u>climped</u> / <u>climbed</u> up the steep mountain.

Kiera <u>wrapped</u> / <u>rhapped</u> a present for her brother.

5 Use the clues to work out each word with <u>silent letters</u>.

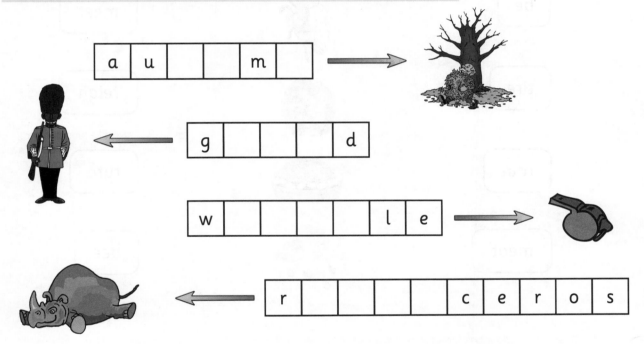

| a | u | | | m | |

| g | | | | d |

| w | | | | | l | e |

| r | | | | | c | e | r | o | s |

6 Write each of these words in a <u>sentence</u>.

biscuit $\Longrightarrow$ ....

castle $\Longrightarrow$ ....

wrist $\Longrightarrow$ ....

Section 16 — Confusing Words

Homophones

Homophones are words that are pronounced the same, but have different meanings and spellings.

pause

You pause when you stop something briefly.

paws

Some animals have paws instead of feet.

---

1 Draw a line to link each picture with the <u>correct word</u>.

be		meet
tire		reign
rain		tyre
meat		bee

---

2 Circle the <u>correct spelling</u> of each word to complete the sentences below.

I am going to <u>write</u> / <u>right</u> a postcard to my aunt Carla.

It's hot outside, <u>so</u> / <u>sew</u> I'm wearing shorts.

Renee and Saif made a <u>fought</u> / <u>fort</u> in Saif's garden.

Grandpa says that he thinks I've <u>groan</u> / <u>grown</u>.

Brody put on the horse's <u>bridal</u> / <u>bridle</u>.

---

3 **Fill in the gaps in the sentences below using the correct words from the box.**

warn / worn   scent / sent   knew / new

My old coat was .... , but I loved the colour.

Mum always wears a perfume with the .... of roses.

There was a sign to .... people about the steep drop.

In November, I will have a .... baby sister.

Mia .... how to set the television to record programmes.

Bo .... back his dinner because it was cold.

4 **The underlined word in each sentence has been spelt incorrectly. Write the correct spelling in the box.**

The boiler was broken, so I looked for a plumber to <u>higher</u>.

Connie <u>kneads</u> to find out what time the auditions start.

The shepherd brought his <u>heard</u> of sheep into the barn.

The <u>whether</u> forecast isn't looking good for the weekend.

5 Circle the word that has been <u>spelt incorrectly</u> in each sentence. Write the <u>correct spelling</u> on the dotted line.

I am going to there house for dinner. ....

We mist our bus, so we will have to walk. ....

My flute lessen went really well today. ....

The teacher asked Denzel to read the story allowed. ....

The recipe needed sugar, butter and flower. ....

6 Fill in the <u>homophones</u> in the boxes below. Then find <u>all</u> the words in the <u>wordsearch</u>.

weak ⟹ | w | e | e | k |

raw ⟹ | r | | | |

hare ⟹ | h | | | |

nit ⟹ | k | | |

would ⟹ | w | | | | |

sum ⟹ | s | | |

```
D H R A W H A R
N I T W E A K W
H A I R L R E O
S F L B I E L U
O W B A W L G L
M E M K N I T D
E E S U M P R O
A K R N R O A R
W W O O D Z R T
```

7 Write a sentence for each of the words in this <u>homophone</u> pair.

which ....

witch ....

Glossary

Adjective — A word that describes a noun, e.g. **clever** girl, **small** box.

Adverb — A word that describes a **verb**, an **adjective** or other **adverbs**.

Adverbial — A group of words that behaves like an **adverb**.

Antonyms — Words that mean the opposite, e.g. **tall** and **short**.

Clause — Part of a sentence that contains a **subject** and a **verb**.

Cohesion — **Linking** ideas together to make your writing **flow smoothly**.

Conjunction — A word or phrase that **joins** two parts of a sentence.

Main clause — A clause that **makes sense** on its own.
e.g. <u>I wash my hands</u> before I eat dinner.

Noun — A word that **names** something, e.g. **Penny**, **nut**, **Bristol**.

Phrase — A group of words usually without a **verb**.

Pronoun — A word used to **replace** a **noun**, e.g. **he**, **you**, **they**.

Subordinate Clause — A clause that **doesn't make sense** on its own.
e.g. I wash my hands <u>before I eat dinner</u>.

Synonyms — Words that mean the same, e.g. **still** and **calm**.

Verb — A doing or being word, e.g. **talk**, **write**, **shout**, **is**.

Glossary

COMMON PUNCTUATION MARKS

Apostrophes — show **missing letters** and **possession**. | `'`

Brackets — **separate extra information** in a sentence. They're also called **parentheses**. | `( )`

Capital letters — used for **starting** sentences and for **names** or **I**. | `A`

Colons — **introduce** some **lists** and **join clauses**. | `:`

Commas — used in **lists**, to **join clauses**, to separate **extra information** and after some **introductions**. | `,`

Dashes — **separate extra information** in a sentence. | `—`

Exclamation marks — show **strong emotions** or **commands**. | `!`

Full stops — show where **sentences end**. | `.`

Hyphens — used to **join words** or **add** a **prefix**. | `-`

Inverted commas — show **direct speech**. They're also called **speech marks**. | `" "`

Question marks — used at the **end** of **questions**. | `?`

Semi-colons — separate **long items** in **lists** and **join clauses**. | `;`

Answers

Grammar

Section 1 — Word Types

Page 4 — Nouns

1. love, pain, kindness, joy, peace
2. The **pride** of lions were lying lazily in the sunshine.
   A **fleet** of ships sailed from England to Africa.
   At the nature reserve, a **herd** of deer ran past me very quickly.
   The children were chased by an angry **swarm** of bees.

Page 5 — Adjectives

1. My grandad baked a **delicious** cake yesterday.
   I bought some **fluffy** slippers to wear at home.
   Matthew found **muddy** boots in the hallway.
   Marina borrowed Shauna's **glittery** pencil case.
   The food was **cold** and people complained.
   The **hungry** football players ate burgers for dinner.
2. Any suitable adjectives.
   Examples:
   The **evil** witches were stirring the potion.
   The diners complimented the chef on his **delicious** food.
   The lady wore a **yellow** scarf to go sledging.
   My **green** coat got **soaked** in the rain.

Page 6 — Verbs

1. Zoë **plays** in the park every weekend.
   They **are** going on holiday to Spain.
   Swimming **relaxes** me after school.
   The dogs **chase** the rabbits around the garden.
   When my dad goes to work, he always **forgets** his lunch.
2. You should have ticked:
   We learn how to do gymnastics in P.E.
   Mr Lewis teaches us about poems.
   They have to draw pictures to give to their parents.

Page 7 — Adverbs

1. Margot was **extremely** pleased with her results.
   Harry bit his lip **nervously** as he looked at the damage.
   The ice cream van plays its music very **loudly**.
   The opera singer got **much** louder as she sang.
   The music stopped **suddenly** and everyone sat down.
2. Paul **never** eats white chocolate because he doesn't like it.
   I love going to the cinema, so I will **definitely** go with you tonight.
   Maria said that she will **probably** come, but she's not sure yet.

Pages 8 and 9 — Modal Verbs

1. You should have ticked:
   He would not come to the party on his own.
   Shanice may be able to join us later.
   We should go downstairs and set the table.
   They must ring the hotel immediately.

2. The plumber **should** fix the radiators.
   We **might** go to the rock concert this weekend.
   I **could** win the race if I train hard enough.
   She **must** answer the phone when it rings.
   We **will** tell the waiter about your allergies.
3. If you are not sure, you **could** ask your teacher.
   I **should** wash my hair but I have run out of shampoo.
   The zebras **must** run quickly to escape the lions.
   You **can** go climbing if you tidy your room first.
   You **should** always put sun cream on at the beach.
   It **might** rain this weekend, but I am not sure.
4. Any suitable sentences.
   Examples:
   You **should** have told me you weren't coming.
   We **must** hurry or we'll be late.
   Alexa **might** play football if she finishes her homework.

Page 10 — Synonyms

1. **caring — kind**, **shout — yell**, **large — big**, **scary — spooky**
2. My mum is **happy** about winning the raffle.
   I was really **sad** about losing my shoes.
   It was just a **typical** day at school.
3. Any suitable synonyms.
   Examples:
   noisy — **loud**, tasty — **delicious**, laugh — **giggle**, neat — **tidy**

Page 11 — Antonyms

1. **take — give**, **exciting — boring**, **create — destroy**, **love — hate**
2. I felt car sick because the road was **twisty**.
   He was really **cowardly** — he should have owned up.
   She was very **generous** and shared her lunch with me.

Page 12 — Pronouns

1. They asked **me** what I thought of the film.
   Sunita and Tom asked **us** if we wanted to eat with them.
   The kind ladies asked if **we** needed any help.
   I need my hammer but I can't find **it** in the shed.
   Lima wanted me to help **her** bake chocolate brownies.
2. Clara likes cheese, so **she** eats a lot of **it**.
   After Elijah ripped the curtains, **he** tried to fix **them**.

Page 13 — Relative Pronouns

1. She found an old car **which** was very rusty.
   We met the actress **who** won the award.
   Shirley baked a cake **which** contained nuts and coffee.
   I have a friend **who** is a firefighter.
2. I bought a jumper **which** was brightly coloured.
   There is a bookshop in town **which** opens on Sundays.
   Tahani adopted a cat **whose** owner had left him.
   The winner is someone **who** has worked very hard.

Answers

Section 2 — Clauses and Sentences

Pages 14 and 15 — Clauses

1. Main clause:
    she read a book
    we baked a cake
    he was in a play
    they sold the painting
    I went to France
    Subordinate clause:
    because it was wet
    after it was over
    who was funny
    if they don't watch
    while they sang

2. You should have underlined these clauses:
    They're making a curry <u>because it's their favourite meal</u>.
    Chidi has two black labradors <u>which are really friendly</u>.
    <u>After the concert ends</u>, we're going to buy some ice-cream.
    I'd like to go for a walk tomorrow <u>even if it's raining</u>.

3. You should have underlined these clauses:
    Ellen, <u>who wants to be a doctor</u>, is going to medical school.
    The museum <u>that stays open at night</u> is very popular.
    The programme <u>that the toddlers were watching</u> was a cartoon.
    My friend, <u>who is called Matt</u>, fell into the pond.
    The old man <u>who lives down the road</u> used to be an actor.

4. The chef **who works in the local café** cooked some ham.
    The kite **that I made with my friend** blew into a tree.
    Jeremy's brother **who loves animals** went to the zoo.
    The statue **which looks like a bear** had fallen over.

Pages 16 and 17 — Sentences

1. Neve took the train down to London. — S
    We went to the shop and I bought some sweets. — C
    Mr and Mrs Adler just moved in next door. — S
    I can't dive, but I want to have some lessons. — C
    Isaac was cold, so he put his coat on. — C

2. We were hungry, **so** we cooked a stew.
    Jaya walked to the beach, **and** she went surfing.
    They wanted to play, **but** the park was shut.

3. Simple:
    They went sailing on the boat.
    Margot's uncle is moving to America.
    Compound:
    He was lost, so he asked for directions.
    We could read or we could watch TV.
    Complex:
    Even though I was tired, I went to see my friend.
    As we watched, the frog jumped out of the pond.

4. Any suitable sentences.
    Examples:
    Simple: The fisherman screamed.
    Compound: The fisherman screamed, and the cow smiled.
    Complex: As the man fished, a cow appeared.

Section 3 — Linking Ideas

Page 18 — Conjunctions

1. Anisa ate a banana **because** she was hungry.
    The milk was out of date, **so** Jo went to the shop.
    The family went to the theatre **and** had a great time.
    I wanted to go to the zoo, **but** it was closed.

2. Marcel likes broccoli, **but** he doesn't like mushrooms.
    There was a storm, **so** we didn't go sailing.

Page 19 — Linking Paragraphs

1. It's very important to eat well and spend time relaxing.
    Firstly, eating healthily means that your body is being looked after from the inside. If you eat well, you will have lots of energy.
    However, don't forget to treat yourself every now and then — it's good for you (not to mention delicious!)
    Secondly, taking time to relax and doing the things you enjoy keeps your mind happy. You should do things that make you feel positive.
    Last of all, it's important to remember that everyone is different. Do what works for you — if exercise make you feel great but your friend prefers knitting, that's okay!

Page 20 — Using Ellipsis

1. You should have matched these pairs:
    They stayed because they were asked. — to stay
    Cara went climbing but Taran didn't. — go climbing
    We visited museums in Poland and Hungary. — we visited museums in
    I like video games but my friends don't. — like video games
    Kimi and Mike bought a house and a dog. — they bought

2. You should have underlined the following words or phrases:
    I need to clean my rugby kit and <u>I need to clean</u> my trainers.
    Talib read about the police dogs and <u>he read about</u> their training.
    This weekend, we should paint the fences and <u>we should paint</u> the shed.
    Sorcha watches programmes about science and <u>programmes about</u> history.

Answers

Section 4 — Tenses

Page 21 — Present Tense and Past Tense

1. I bought a new hat for the wedding. — past
   Samir does his homework after dinner. — present
   We listened to our favourite song. — past
   Toby went on holiday to France. — past
   Remi goes to dance class on Tuesdays. — present

2. Laura <u>visits</u> the island. — Laura **visited** the island.
   The dog <u>rolls</u> over. — The dog **rolled** over.
   I <u>eat</u> lunch at midday. — I **ate** lunch at midday.
   We finish at 3 o'clock. — We **finished** at 3 o'clock.

Page 22 — Verbs with 'ing'

1. You **are shouting** for Li.
   I **am baking** a pie.
   They **are moving** house.
   Amy **is looking** for you.

2. You should be left with:
   I **was** watching the film.
   You **were** telling the story.
   She **was** taking the bus.
   They **were** singing along.

Pages 23 and 24 — Verbs with 'have'

1. Dominic **has** passed his test.
   I **have** done my chores.
   You **have** worked hard.
   Riley and Priya **have** made clay sculptures.
   Maisie **has** been in the garden.

2. Olivia **has asked** to go first.
   We **have found** the recipe.
   Hassan **has saved** his pocket money.

3. You should have ticked these sentences:
   Will had received the letter.
   They had brought the map.
   I had drawn the picture myself.

4. They **had stopped**.
   He **had hurt** his knee.
   She **had thrown** the ball.
   Max **had missed** the bus.

Page 25 — Staying in the Same Tense

1. Dan goes home and watches television before he eats dinner.
   I am getting cold because I am not wearing a coat even though it is snowing.
   Amir rang Lucy and invited her to his birthday party because they were friends.

2. You should have circled and corrected these words:
   I **build** a huge... — built
   I **work** on it... — worked
   I **stop** for an... — stopped
   and **knocks** it down! — knocked

Section 5 — Sentence Structure

Pages 26 and 27 — Subject and Object

1. <u>Hanifa</u> goes to school.
   <u>The builder</u> bought a ladder.
   <u>The bananas</u> changed colour.
   <u>Donna</u> made an apple pie.

2. We painted **the fences**.
   I cooked **eggs** this morning.
   Pandas eat **bamboo**.
   Chesleigh climbed **the wall**.

3. a letter — object
   The lizard — subject
   Dinosaurs — subject
   his racket — object

4. The parrot repeated **the question**. — object
   Tony went to the waterpark. — subject
   The cricket players won **the match**. — object
   Dolphins are playful animals. — subject

5. Any suitable sentences.
   Examples:
   Robbie took **his lunch** from his bag.
   Carys dropped her phone in the pool.
   Romain chased the vampire away.
   Sarah played with **the hamster**.
   Camels live in the desert.
   They bought **new shoes** for the dance.

Pages 28 and 29 — Passive and Active Voice

1. Active sentences:
   We bought new umbrellas.
   The dog ate her sandwich.
   He painted the puppets.
   Shane fell in the ditch.
   Passive sentences:
   The card was written by Tia.
   The key was lost by Sammy.
   Their cat was found by me.
   The bus was delayed by a flood.

2. You should have ticked these sentences:
   The motorcycles were driven by professionals.
   The dam was built by the beavers.
   The jumper was knitted by my grandad.

3. The pie was eaten by George.
   The parcel was delivered by Faisal.
   The rabbit was adopted by Wendy.

4. The sentences should have been rewritten as follows:
   The suitcase was picked up by Candice.
   The medal was won by the best athlete.
   The ball was passed to Hannah by Kai.

Answers

Section 6 — Writing Style

Pages 30 to 32 — Formal and Informal Writing

1. I'm starving. — I
    I am extremely hungry. — F
    She is annoying me. — F
    She's getting on my nerves. — I
    Please hurry up. — F
    Just get a move on. — I
    Take your hands off it! — I
    Do not touch it. — F

2. Thank you for replying to my letter. — formal writing
    That action film was so cool. — informal writing
    We were gutted with the score. — informal writing
    The test was extremely difficult. — formal writing
    I scoffed all the biscuits. — informal writing

3. You should have matched these pairs:
    That can't be right. — That cannot be true.
    I wish it was that simple. — I wish it were that simple.
    You're coming, aren't you? — Are you coming?

4. You should have ticked these sentences:
    We had an enjoyable day at the beach.
    He would play outside if it were warmer.
    Nobody believed I would go to the party.

5. You should have circled the words in bold:
    The food at the restaurant was **terrible**.
    We were all **tired** after the match.
    I saw her **steal** your pencil case.
    He is **bored** of playing that game.
    Diego was **eager** to know the answer.
    The teacher thought they were **clever**.

6. Across: 1: hurried
    2: crying
    3: threw
    Down: 1: thought
    2: carried
    3: friend

Pages 33 and 34 — Writing for Your Audience

1. You should have ticked these sentences:
    A letter to your local newspaper.
    A school report about World War II.

2. A thank you note to your uncle. — informal writing
    A science report for school. — formal writing
    A letter to your headteacher. — formal writing
    A party invitation to your friend. — informal writing
    An essay about the Romans. — formal writing
    An email to your cousin. — informal writing

3. You should have ticked these sentences:
    An article in a newspaper — Police are still looking for the criminal.
    A postcard to your friend — I'm having an awesome time!
    A letter of complaint — I expect you to fix it.
    A note to your dad — I'm sorry for shouting at you.

4. You should have ticked these sentences:
    It would be wonderful if you were to visit our school.
    I look forward to hearing from you.

Pages 35 to 37 — Standard and Non-Standard English

1. Clara ran into the garden. — Standard English
    I is not listening anymore. — non-Standard English
    You done everything wrong. — non-Standard English
    He is very happy to see you. — Standard English
    We was going to the supermarket. — non-Standard English
    Those chocolates is very tasty. — non-Standard English
    I did my homework before going out. — Standard English

2. You should have matched these pairs:
    She could of come with us. — She could have come with us.
    You would of upset them. — You would have upset them.
    He should of phoned me. — He should have phoned me.

3. You should have crossed out these words:
    I (~~seen~~ / saw) the dog steal the sausages.
    Ben (did / ~~done~~) all his work.
    We (~~gone~~ / went) out before Lucy arrived.
    They (~~come~~ / came) to the concert last night.
    I (drank / ~~drunk~~) all the milk.
    You (~~swum~~ / swam) further than I did.

4. I think ___ flowers belong to her. — those
    Pick up ___ clothes for me. — those
    It was nice of ___ to visit us. — them
    She likes ___ cakes over there. — those
    Have you told ___ the news? — them
    I don't want to talk to ___ . — them

5. Harry got into trouble for hitting **me**.
    My friends and **I** play hockey.
    My brother gave **me** this jumper.
    I told you not to, but you didn't listen.

6. I haven't eaten nothing today. — 2
    Joe didn't see any animals on safari. — 1
    I wasn't going to tell nobody. — 2
    Kerry couldn't see nothing outside. — 2
    I don't have anything to say. — 1

7. Any suitable sentences that use correct grammar.
    Examples:
    He hasn't seen anybody.
    They aren't with us.
    You haven't done anything.
    I haven't got any pens.
    We aren't going to do it.

Answers

Punctuation

Section 7 — Sentence Punctuation

Page 38 — Capital Letters and Full Stops

1. You should have ticked these sentences:
   Cornwall is a popular holiday destination.
   Fleur has lived in both France and England.
   You should have crossed these sentences:
   Jan wants to visit a museum in germany.
   my cousin hollie is getting married in may.
   Football and Netball are team Sports

2. **J**ack and **K**yle skateboard in **H**yde **P**ark.
   Elisha is in **M**rs **P**atel's class next year.
   I have a black and white dog called **L**ola.

Page 39 — Question Marks and Exclamation Marks

1. What's your favourite colour — **?**
   Dinner was alright — **.**
   Can you help me — **?**
   Let's see what happens — **.**
   I don't know who to ask — **.**
   Whose shoes are those — **?**
   Who wants to play a game — **?**
   Our family is quite small — **.**
   Are you finished — **?**
   We'd better get going now — **.**

2. We're having pizza tonight**.**
   Wow, I can't wait**!**
   My socks are green**.**
   Oh, what a beautiful day**!**
   Quick, somebody help me**!**
   Pass the sugar, please**.**

3. Any suitable sentences which use punctuation correctly.
   Example:
   Can I have a piece of that cake**?**

Pages 40 and 41 — Sentence Practice

1. You should have circled the following letters:
   The river in **L**ondon is called the **T**hames.
   Wales is a country in **G**reat **B**ritain.
   Charles **D**arwin was a famous scientist.

2. Ouch, that hurt — **!**
   Where are we — **?**
   Who is that — **?**
   Kai took a photo — **.**
   Meg asks for help — **.**
   Wow, yes please — **!**
   Oh no, look out — **!**
   Is it raining — **?**

3. You should have ticked these sentences:
   I never said that!
   What did you do in Scotland?
   You should have crossed these sentences:
   I saw a magician at the circus?
   What? does Zadie like to eat!
   What game did Dylan buy.

4. Izzy was doing tricks on her bike.
   "Watch this**!**" she shouted to Charlie.
   "What are you doing**?**" Charlie asked.
   "You'll see!" she replied**.**
   She jumped**.** The bike flew through the air like a bird.
   "That's amazing**!**" Charlie cried out.

5. Any suitable sentences which use punctuation correctly.
   Examples:
   Ouch, I wasn't expecting that**!**
   Chloe put on her roller skates**.**
   Who put that paint pot there**?**

Section 8 — Commas

Page 42 — Commas in Lists

1. You should have ticked:
   I can't eat peanuts, almonds or hazelnuts.
   My new trousers are blue, purple, orange and pink.
   Steve's cats are called Tiger, Arnold and Mr Fluffs.
   My dad plays the guitar, the violin and the flute.

2. I add raspberries, blueberries and grapes to my yoghurt.
   I can't find my pencil, my rubber or my highlighter.
   My dog, my cat, my parrot and my fish all get along very well.
   The thieves stole two forks, a plate, some butter and my duvet.

Page 43 — Commas to Avoid Confusion

1. When can we eat, Alexander?
   I don't like fighting, spiders or bananas.
   Anaya loves painting, elephants and hockey.
   Our Christmas involves mince pies, singing carols and presents.

2. Any sensible explanation.
   Example:
   The first sentence tells you that I only helped two people find the treasure. The second sentence tells you that I helped three people find the treasure.

Answers

Page 44 — Commas After Subordinate Clauses

1. You should have ticked:
   As the lions slept, the zebras ran away.
   While the cake was baking, we made the icing.

2. When you come round later, we could watch a film.
   I will tell the truth even if I get in trouble.
   She wasn't listening while I explained the instructions.
   Since I was in Newcastle, I went to see the Angel of the North.

Page 45 — Commas After Introductions

1. In the future, I'd like to learn how to fix cars.
   Earlier this week, I went to visit my nephew.
   As quietly as she could, Mary left the room.
   In the rainforest, you can find lots of different animals.
   On Sunday evening, we cooked a delicious roast dinner.

2. At the weekend, I like to go walking in the hills.
   In Brazil, there is a big festival called Carnival.
   On Thursdays, I play hockey after school.

Pages 46 and 47 — Commas for Extra Information

1. Hamsters, which are a type of rodent, are very friendly.
   The basket, which was full of eggs, fell on the floor.
   Sam, who is my cousin, passed his piano exam.
   The museum, which was built in 1904, is still very popular.
   We bumped into Kim, our tennis coach, at the supermarket.
   Everest, the highest mountain in the world, is very difficult to climb.

2. You should have ticked:
   The milkman, who works on Mondays, is very friendly.
   The café, which serves delicious food, won an award.
   Ceara's grandma, who is very kind, made us all dinner.

3. We saw some penguins, my favourite animal, at the zoo.
   Alana's house, which is next door to mine, has a swimming pool.
   My friend, who is from Belgium, speaks French and German.
   The Amazon river, found in South America, is over 4,000 miles long.
   I am going to York, where my grandparents live, for the weekend.
   Big Ben, which is in London, is a famous building.
   Your cousin, who is a policeman, is coming into school.

4. The apple, which had fallen from the tree, was bruised.
   Our tent, which is very old, has holes in the top.
   The sandwich, which I only bought yesterday, is already mouldy.

Pages 48 and 49 — Comma Practice

1. You need to shave, Max. — to avoid confusion
   At the start, we all sat in a circle and said our names. — after an adverbial phrase
   Olivia, who is a singer, loves performing on stage. — to add extra information
   Gorillas, leopards, monkeys and snakes live in the jungle. — separating items in a list

2. After hugging, Ted, James and Melissa left the party.
   Shall we draw, Kitty?

3. You should have ticked:
   I went to the cinema with Esme, David and Regina.
   The old building, which had been abandoned, was unsafe.
   Next winter, I am going skiing with my family.

4. The underlined commas aren't needed:
   The suitcase, was very heavy, so I struggled to carry it.
   We went to the bank, the post office, and the bakery.
   My shoelaces got tangled, together, and I fell over.
   Next summer, I'd like to go camping, with my friends.
   Christmas Island, near Australia, is home, to millions of red crabs.

5. When I go on holiday, I like to play on the beach.
   Before you answer the questions, read the instructions carefully.
   As I left the building, I saw my mum waiting.

Section 9 — Brackets and Dashes

Page 50 — Brackets for Extra Information

1. Mr Mysterious (a famous magician) performed an incredible trick.
   The bus driver (a cheerful, elderly man) chatted to the children.
   Heidi the hamster (the class pet) escaped from her cage.
   Victor's shoes (a pair of trainers) were chewed by the dog.
   I found it (the stolen chocolate bar) in Tammy's room.

2. I saw her (the school bully) shouting at the boys.
   Franco's Place (my favourite restaurant) is always busy.
   The teacher's car (an orange one) was parked on the street.
   Emily's aunt (a television presenter) came to our school.
   The book (a travel guide) is on the top shelf.

Page 51 — Dashes for Extra Information

1. You should have ticked these sentences:
   The toad — brown and warty — sat on the rock.
   The pirate — the ship's captain — shouted at the crew.

Answers

2. Nobody — not even Martin — could solve the puzzle.
   The chicks — cold and helpless — huddled together.
   The houses — the new ones next to the river — were flooded.

3. The actor — an Australian — won the award.

Page 52 — Single Dashes

1. You should have ticked these sentences:
   The cat ran across the lawn — the birds flew away.
   The sun shone brightly — it was a beautiful day.
   Iona tripped over the branch — she hit the floor hard.

2. You should have left in these dashes:
   The school bell rang — it was time to go home.
   Smoke poured out of the kitchen — something was burning.
   Eliza looked out of the window — it was snowing heavily.
   I paused the film — I could hear something upstairs.
   The teacher spilled his tea — the children laughed.

Page 53 — Hyphens

1. She hates high-heeled shoes.
   The red-winged insect flew away.
   That is a short-clawed lizard.
   I have lots of long-sleeved shirts.

2. My cat **recovered** quickly after her operation.
   The teacher had to **re-mark** the children's tests.

Section 10 — Apostrophes

Page 54 — Apostrophes for Missing Letters

1. Kirsty **couldn't** come today.
   You'd like the view from the hills.
   You're late because you overslept.
   Do you think **I'm** funny?

2. They'll know what to do. — **They will**
   She could've asked for help. — **could have**
   He hadn't found his wallet. — **had not**
   I'd forgotten his name. — **I had**
   Seb didn't like chopping onions. — **did not**

Page 55 — Its and It's

1. You should have ticked these sentences:
   It's been a lovely afternoon at the beach.
   The shop opened its doors at nine o'clock.

2. I don't think that **it's** a big problem.
   A spider catches flies in **its** web.
   It's been snowing in the mountains.
   Dad's car has a lot of space in **its** boot.
   It's taken a long time to get here.
   It's great to see you!

Page 56 — Apostrophes for Possession

1. my school**'s** field
   the girl**'s** ball
   Jo**'s** hamster
   the bus**'s** bell
   Rome**'s** ruins

2. the cars' wheels
   the songs' words
   the games' rules
   the classes' pens
   the cakes' candles

Page 57 — Apostrophe Practice

1. You should have crossed these sentences and corrected these words:
   Lets' go to the beach today. — **Let's**
   Your'e going to come with us. — **You're**
   I wou'ldve liked to visit the zoo. — **would've**
   Theyd' been to visit Anais. — **They'd**

2. My **mum's** name is Karina and she works in an office.
   We ate at **Paris's** most popular restaurant.
   The **house's** garden was wild and full of weeds.
   A guide told the **museum's** visitors to be quiet.

3. Any suitable sentence.
   Example:
   The monkey scratched **its** head.

Section 11 — Inverted Commas

Pages 58 and 59 — Punctuating Speech

1. You should have ticked these sentences:
   "I want beans on toast for breakfast," said Camille.
   "Who here," said the teacher, "has done the homework?"

2. Paolo asked, "<u>w</u>hen will dinner be ready?" — missing capital letter
   "I never make mistakes<u>"</u> said Professor Stirling. — missing punctuation
   "Before you go," said Trisha, "you must meet him"<u>.</u> — punctuation in the wrong place
   "This is utterly disgraceful"<u>!</u> shouted Freda. — punctuation in the wrong place

3. "Turn the music down!" shouted Jodi's neighbour.
   George asked, **"**What should I do about it?**"**
   "Let's go to the beach," said Eve, **"**because it's a lovely day.**"**
   "Give me the car keys," said Sandrine, **"**as I'm late for work.**"**

4. Darcy shouted**,** "Leave me alone!"
   "I want to see Buckingham Palace**,**" said Lin.
   "Who wants to watch a film tonight**?**" asked Peter**.**
   "The problem is," said Humphrey**,** "we don't know where it is.**"**
   Mason said, **"**I don't like broccoli, but I love biscuits**.**"

Answers

5. "When are we going to set off?" asked Rupert.
   "Here are the results of the experiment," announced Kyle.

Pages 60 and 61 — Direct and Reported Speech

1. They said they would be here. — reported speech
   "I don't understand," said Terry. — direct speech
   "Can you pass me the salt?" asked Greta. — direct speech
   He told me you wanted to leave. — reported speech
   Yuri yelled, "Listen to me!" — direct speech
   I heard Michal say he likes jazz music. — reported speech

2. You should have ticked these sentences:
   I bought you flowers, said Gary, and some chocolates.
   What a beautiful gift! said Marie.

3. Direct speech: "My pigs have escaped!"
   "When does it open?"
   "I went to the museum."
   Indirect speech: He asked for directions.
   They talked about the film.
   She said she was tired.

4. You should have ticked these sentences:
   Lucas said he's going swimming this weekend.
   My best friend says we can go with them tomorrow.
   Neil told me it was closed, but I don't believe him.
   She had asked to play outside, but she wasn't allowed.
   You should have added these inverted commas:
   "Don't forget to water all the plants," said Mum.
   "Nobody move," whispered the explorer, "and keep quiet."
   "I like painting," I heard him say.

Section 12 — Colons and Semi-Colons

Pages 62 and 63 — Colons

1. You should have ticked these sentences:
   Tyrese has three best friends: Asher, Talisha and Lee.
   I enjoy the creative subjects: music, art, dance and drama.

2. Any suitable sentences that use punctuation correctly. Examples:
   Hari picks his outfit: a red jacket, some blue jeans and a pair of brown boots.
   I packed my favourite things: my hat, sunglasses, camera and book.

3. You should have left in these colons:
   I can't buy that beautiful necklace: it's too expensive.
   Rosa went home at 5 o'clock: she needed to be back before dark.
   Alan laughed at Oskar's joke: Oskar told the best jokes.
   Tell Susi that I'll be late: the train hasn't arrived yet.

4. I am going to put on suncream: it's really sunny.
   Tegan gave her green sweets to me: she hates them.
   Rupert does know Riley: they're cousins.
   I'll go to the shop tomorrow: it's getting late now.

5. I hope it's lunchtime soon: I'm hungry.
   I love the monkey bars: I'm really good at them.
   We have to go to school: it's Monday.

Pages 64 and 65 — Semi-Colons

1. You should have ticked these sentences:
   My bike is yellow; my sister's bike is green.
   Dad is thirty-nine; Uncle George is forty-one.
   Simon likes playing snap; Lily prefers chess.

2. Anya walks to school; Liam gets the bus.
   Syed likes strawberries; Lacey likes plums.

3. I own one lazy, old dog called Rascal; two kittens, which I got from the shelter; and a rabbit with floppy ears.
   School dinner was either pepperoni pizza and potato wedges; a jacket potato with beans, which was the vegetarian option; or a hot, spicy chilli.
   The painter painted a castle, which was in ruins; some tall, snowy mountains; and a dark green forest in moonlight.

4. At the school bake sale, Zak sold six cupcakes, which had cherries on top; three delicious, crunchy chocolate chip cookies; and one whole apple pie.

Pages 66 and 67 — Colons and Semi-Colons Practice

1. There are three choices of pizza: cheese, pepperoni or mushroom.
   At the campsite, I set up the three-person tent; I started a fire, which took a while; and I roasted some marshmallows.
   My cat had four kittens: Tiger, Bella, Ginger and Socks.

2. You should have joined these statements:
   Sasha played inside — it was raining.
   I ran 10 miles this week — I'm preparing for a marathon.
   Kobi won the game — he rolled a six.
   We must buy a ticket today — the show will sell out quickly.

3. I keep reptiles: snakes, turtles and lizards.
   We have two trees: one with soft, ripe pears and one with spiky conkers.

4. On Tuesdays, I play squash; on Fridays, I play tennis.
   Charlotte likes peas; she doesn't like sweetcorn.
   Talia plays the clarinet; Shane plays the flute.
   This flight is to Japan; that one is to Australia.
   Clocks go forward in spring; they go back in autumn.
   Elliot got six questions right; Matt got four questions right.

Answers

Section 13 — Paragraphs and Layout

Pages 68 and 69 — Paragraphs

1. "Let's go to the boxing class," suggested Emma. "I'd rather try karate," replied Sam. — A new person is speaking.
   Sona and Jim live in Barnam. In Nessington, there is a grand stadium. — A different place is mentioned.
   The team met for practice at 10 am. At 3 pm, the tournament began. — The time has changed.
   The children are starting to settle down. My cat hasn't been very well recently. — A new subject has been introduced.

2. Any suitable sentences.
   Examples:
   I fell off my bike.
   It's going to be sunny and hot every day.

3. You should have added these paragraph markers:
   We were heading inside for the night when we heard a noise coming from the end of the garden. // "Take your sister inside," said Dad, already moving towards the noise. // "But Dad, I want to come with you!" I protested. // "It's probably just a bird. If it's exciting I'll call you, I promise," he said, smiling, as he strolled down the path towards the bushes. // As we got to the door, I heard Dad shout, "Girls, come quickly! You need to see this!"

4. Any suitable explanations.
   Examples:
   2nd paragraph: new subject
   3rd paragraph: change of time
   4th paragraph: new person speaking

Page 70 — Layout Devices

1. 1. heading
   2. subheading
   3. bullet points
   4. table
   5. box

Page 71 — Writing Lists

1. • trustworthy
   • honest
   • a good listener

2. Any list of three items using numbered lists correctly.
   Example:
   2) wash my face
   3) eat my breakfast
   4) get ready for school

Spelling

Section 14 — Prefixes

Page 72 — Prefixes — 'under' 'over' 'en' and 'em'

1. Let's find a cheaper vase — this one is **over**priced.
   My broccoli turned to mush because it was **over**cooked.
   Don't **under**estimate her abilities — she's very clever.
   If I **over**eat, I feel too full and get a stomach ache.
   My friends don't like it, but I think the film is **under**appreciated.
   Shauni is very tired because she is **over**worked.

2. to hire — **employ**
   make angry — **enrage**
   make possible — **enable**
   hug — **embrace**
   put a spell on — **enchant**

Page 73 — Prefixes — 'mid' 'pre' 'fore' and 'non'

1. **midair**
   preview
   foreground
   nonsense

2. I always have a cup of tea and a slice of cake at **mid**day.
   The weather **fore**cast is good for this weekend.
   The bread didn't take long to cook because it was **pre**baked.
   The dog had been barking **non**stop all day.
   My **fore**head hurts because I banged it when I fell over.
   They reached the **mid**point in their journey.

Pages 74 and 75 — Prefixes — 'bi' 'tri' and 'semi'

1. You should have ticked these sentences:
   A trimonthly event happens three times a month.
   Something with three colours is tricolour.
   My sister is a semiprofessional athlete.
   A tripod is a structure with three legs.

2. **semifinal**, **tricycle**, **semidry**, **tripart**, **biweekly**

3. **binoculars**
   triangle
   bicycle
   biplane
   semicircle

4. I live in a **semidetached** house.
   The **biannual** trip happens twice a year.
   They moved to a **semirural** town.
   My mum is now **semiretired**.

Answers

Section 15 — Word Endings and Suffixes

Pages 76 and 77 — Word Endings — the 'shus' sound

1. You should have circled: **precious, infectious, delicious, ambitious.**
   Eva cooked a **delicious** meal last night.
   Mila's ring was very **precious** to her.
   The builders had **ambitious** plans for the garden.
   I picked up an **infectious** disease on holiday.

2. My cat is quite gentle — she isn't mali**cious**.
   The characters in the book aren't real — they are ficti**tious**.
   Vegetables are full of vitamins — they're nutri**tious**.
   Swans can be vi**cious** if you go near their nest.
   I think black cats bring bad luck — I am supersti**tious**.

3. Words ending 'cious': **gracious, conscious, ferocious**
   Words ending 'tious': **fractious, overambitious, contentious**

4. The restaurant's food was absolutely **atrocious**.
   I didn't want to sound **ungracious**.
   The apple pie was utterly **scrumptious**.
   There had been plenty of rain, so the grass was **luscious**.
   The police found a **suspicious** car in the woods.
   The doctor helped the woman who was **unconscious**.

5. Any suitable sentence.
   Examples:
   I am **cautious** around my neighbour's dog.
   My bedroom is very **spacious**.

Pages 78 and 79 — Word Endings — the 'shul' sound

1. **crucial, racial, confidential, facial**

2. You should have circled: **torrential, beneficial, martial, residential**
   We got soaked in the **torrential** rain.
   They live on a quiet **residential** estate.
   My older sister takes **martial** art classes.
   Running is very **beneficial** for your health.

3. The criminal stole their **financial** information.
   The police received reports of **antisocial** behaviour.
   David's first **initial** is 'D'.
   Cole has the **potential** to be a great baseball player.
   Auntie Sue gave me **impartial** advice on my problem.

4. **official, essential, social**

5. You should have ticked: **special, artificial**
   Any suitable sentences.
   Examples:
   They organised a **special** surprise for my birthday.
   There is an **artificial** plant in the kitchen.

Pages 80 and 81 — Word Endings — 'ant' and 'ent'

1. Words ending 'ant': **distant, mutant, brilliant**
   Words ending 'ent': **silent, decent, patient**

2. The explorers made a **significant** discovery.
   My work is **consistent**, so my teachers are pleased.
   I'm learning a new dance for the school **talent** show.
   There was an **incident** at school today.
   I wasn't sure, so I was **hesitant** to put my hand up.

3. **arrogant, comment, tolerant**

4. eleph**ant**, presid**ent**, differ**ent**, assist**ant**

5. I live on the contin**ent** of Europe.
   Priya can talk to anyone — she is more confid**ent** than me.
   I always try to be kind and pleas**ant** when I meet new people.
   Olly is very intellig**ent** — he got full marks in his exams.
   Sunita does things for herself because she is independ**ent**.
   I bought a fragr**ant** candle that smells like black cherry.

Pages 82 and 83 — Word Endings — 'ance', 'ancy' and 'ence, 'ency'

1. You should have underlined: **consequence, guidance, infancy, agency, decency, resistance**

2. import**ance**, appli**ance**, expect**ancy**, obedi**ence**, frequ**ency**

3. The policeman asked to see my driving **licence**.
   Bianca's mum is taking part in an **endurance** race.
   He has a **tendency** to sleep through his morning alarms.
   The **attendance** at the football match was fantastic.
   She asked me to deliver the parcel as a matter of **urgency**.
   The lawyer tried to prove the man's **innocence**.

4. Across: 1. currency
           2. confidence
           3. advance
   Down: 1. vacancy
         2. emergency
         3. pregnancy

Pages 84 and 85 — Word Endings — 'able' and 'ible'

1. Correct spelling: **laughable, incredible, available, payable, reasonable**
   Incorrect spelling: **laughible, incredable, availible, payible, reasonible**

2. The cake went mouldy, so it was no longer **edible**.
   My brother isn't very **likeable** — he's really mean to me.
   Doing gymnastics has made me very **flexible**.
   My best friend is always happy and **excitable**.
   Going to bed early is **preferable** to staying up late.

Answers

I haven't drunk enough water, so I have a **terrible** headache.

Our new sofa is more **comfortable** than our old one.

3. **adorable**, **possible**, **sizeable**

4. **reversible**, **suitable**, **visible**, **capable**, **believable**

5. The most desir**able** chocolates in a box are eaten first.

"You can't beat me," shouted the villain, "I'm invinc**ible**!"

Stefani likes to wear very fashion**able** clothes.

They threw me a surprise party, and it was really enjoy**able**.

She tried to be quiet, but we could all hear her very aud**ible** whisper.

Marc doesn't like celery — he thinks it tastes horr**ible**.

Pages 86 and 87 — Word Endings — 'ably' and 'ibly'

1. Words ending 'ably': **admirably**, **predictably**
Words ending 'ibly': **forcibly**, **irresponsibly**

2. **disagreeably**, **irritably**, **favourably**, **probably**, **irresistibly**

3. **possibly**, **terribly**, **reliably**

4. Last Thursday, it was **unbearably** hot.
The thief, dressed in black, ran **invisibly** through the streets.
Karen is mature and always acts **responsibly**.
In the video game, the car was spinning **uncontrollably**.

5. The children all behaved sens**ibly** on the school trip.
The skyscraper they have built seems imposs**ibly** tall.
They didn't win, but the girls were argu**ably** the best relay team.
Our kitchen is consider**ably** more modern than it used to be.
My local rugby team played reason**ably** well at the weekend.

Pages 88 and 89 — Adding Suffixes to Words Ending in 'fer'

1. **preference**, **reference**, **indifference**

2. Leila was **offering** her sweets to the class.
I was **referring** to my hamster, not my guinea pig.
I chose the window seat, **preferring** to look outside.
Toma was **suffering** from a headache.
We had **differing** opinions on what we wanted to eat.

3. differ**ence**, infer**ence**, confer**ence**

4. You should have circled: **preferred**, **referred**, **transferred**
The vet **referred** to my cat by the wrong name.
We **transferred** our luggage from the house to the car.
When I was younger, I **preferred** the colour yellow.

5. You should have ticked: **offered**, **suffered**
Any suitable sentences.
Examples:
Abed **offered** his car to Troy.
I **suffered** an injury playing rugby.

Section 16 — Confusing Words

Pages 90 and 91 — 'ei' and 'ie' Words

1. th**ie**f, dec**ei**ve, rec**ei**ve, p**ie**ce

2. You should have ticked: **shield** and **neighbour**.
You should have crossed: **wieght**, **soceity**, **cieling** and **acheive**.

3. br**ie**f, n**ei**gh, r**ei**gn, bel**ie**ve, f**ie**rce, misch**ie**f

4. You should have circled: **wierd**, **hieght**, **retreive** and **anceint**.

5. ei: **neither**, **deceit**, **either**
ie: **nutrient**, **diesel**, **pier**

6. You should have circled these words:
Edmund **seized** the ball and ran.
My **friend** is moving to Manchester.
Eggs are good sources of **protein**.
Tea and coffee are high in **caffeine**.

Pages 92 and 93 — Words with 'ough' in

1. dough

2. words with an 'uff' sound: **enough**, **rough**, **tough**
words with an 'ow' sound: **drought**, **bough**
words with an 'or' sound: **brought**, **bought**, **sought**

3. **thorough** and **borough**
dough and **though**
sought and **ought**

4. something you do when you're ill — **cough**
another word for 'zero' — **nought**
the opposite of smooth — **rough**
another word for 'argued' — **fought**
part of a tree — **bough**
another word for 'strong' — **tough**

5. Michael **bought** a souvenir on holiday.
Although I was tired, I worked hard.
The train went **through** a tunnel.
I **ought** to go to sleep early tonight.
There wasn't **enough** time to score another goal.

6. Any suitable sentences.
Example:
The tractor pulls a **plough**.
I **thought** I would go into town today.

Pages 94 and 95 — Words with Silent Letters

1. plum**b**er, **h**our, ca**l**m, lis**t**en, **g**narled, **k**nee, solem**n**, i**s**land

2. ghost — **h**, watch — **t**, column — **n**, sign — **g**, guitar — **u**, honest — **h**

Answers

3. Silent c words: **scissors**, **scene**
   Silent h words: **whale**, **vehicle**
   Silent n words: **hymn**, **condemn**
   Silent w words: **sword**, **wrong**

4. You should have circled these words:
   On his trip to the farm, Rahul saw a cow and its **calf**.
   The dog **gnawed** on its rubber bone.
   There were some daisies among the **thistles**.
   The goat **climbed** up the steep mountain.
   Kiera **wrapped** a present for her brother.

5. **autumn**, **guard**, **whistle**, **rhinoceros**

6. Any suitable sentences.
   Examples:
   I took a ginger **biscuit** from the jar.
   A dragon guarded the **castle**.
   Nadira broke her **wrist** playing hockey.

Pages 96 to 98 — Homophones

1. You should have linked these words to their pictures:

   bee   tyre

   meat   rain

2. You should have circled these words:
   I am going to **write** a postcard to my aunt Carla.
   It's hot outside, **so** I'm wearing shorts.
   Renee and Saif made a **fort** in Saif's garden.
   Grandpa says that he thinks I've **grown**.
   Brody put on the horse's **bridle**.

3. My old coat was **worn**, but I loved the colour.
   Mum always wears a perfume with the **scent** of roses.
   There was a sign to **warn** people about the steep drop.
   In November, I will have a **new** baby sister.
   Mia **knew** how to set the television to record programmes.
   Bo **sent** back his dinner because it was cold.

4. higher — **hire**
   kneads — **needs**
   heard — **herd**
   whether — **weather**

5. I am going to <u>there</u> house for dinner. — **their**
   We <u>mist</u> our bus, so we will have to walk. — **missed**
   My flute <u>lessen</u> went really well today. — **lesson**
   The teacher asked Denzel to read the story <u>allowed</u>. — **aloud**
   The recipe needed sugar, butter and <u>flower</u>. — **flour**

6. raw — **roar**, hare — **hair**, nit — **knit**, would — **wood**, sum — **some**

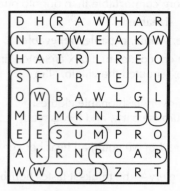

7. Any suitable sentence.
   Examples:
   Which cup is mine?
   The **witch** flew on her broomstick.